GROWING GOOD INFLUENCE

10 PERSONAL BARRIERS ORDINARY PEOPLE OVERCOME TO CULTIVATE EXTRAORDINARY INFLUENCE

TOM GREENTREE

Copyright © 2019 Tom Greentree
All rights reserved.
print ISBN: 9781999530907
ebook ISBN: 9781999530914
audiobook ISBN: 9781999530921

No part of this publication may be reproduced, distributed, or transmitted in any form or by any means, including photocopying, recording, or other electronic or mechanical methods, without the prior written permission of the publisher, except in the case of brief quotations embodied in reviews and certain other non-commercial uses permitted by copyright law.

Cover Design © 2019 pro_ebookcovers

Author Headshot © 2018 @daylewiens

Scripture quotations marked NLT are taken from the *Holy Bible*, New Living Translation, copyright © 1996, 2004, 2015 by Tyndale House Foundation. Used by permission of Tyndale House Publishers, Inc., Carol Stream, Illinois 60188. All rights reserved.

Scripture quotations marked NIV are taken from THE HOLY BIBLE, NEW INTERNATIONAL VERSION®, NIV® Copyright © 1973, 1978, 1984, 2011 by Biblica, Inc.® Used by permission. All rights reserved worldwide.

Please note: Because the author is Canadian, many of the spellings are Canadian as well: neighbour instead of neighbor, favour rather than favor —that sort of thing. If a word seems like it's arranged a little different, chalk it up to the northern climes and favour this Canadian neighbour with grace.

CONTENTS

Introduction vii

Section One 1
1. Integrity 3
2. Knowledge 33
3. Humility 63
Section Two 81
4. Empathy 83
5. Respect 103
6. Grace 125
7. Love 143
Section Three 161
8. Vision 163
9. Positivity 181
10. Patience 205

A Final Word 223
Acknowledgments 225
About the Author 227

I dedicate this book to my good influencers. First, to Doug Greentree, my father, who passed away during the final stages of this book's completion (though not before reading an advance copy). My dad embodied the kind of character outlined in these pages, and no one has had greater influence in my life. I'm thankful to God for him.

Second, I dedicate this book to others who've surrounded me through the years, especially Gerald, Waldie, Ian, Alan, and Jon. If you see yourself in these pages, it's because of who you've been to me and how you've shaped who I am. I owe you more than I can say.

Thank you.

INTRODUCTION

We have the power to help or to hurt others. I suspect you agree. And I'm struck by how much that help or hurt flows from who we are personally. Our attitudes, our practices, our theology, and our character all affect our ability to help others grow.

You can think of examples, I'm sure. People in a position to help others, able to offer a perspective shift, a new insight, a Jesus introduction, or a terrific opportunity but *because of something in them* (an unidentified attitude, an unhelpful practice, or a character deficiency) they render their influence negligible. Or worse, even harmful.

Due to personal blind spots, they are unable to bring the hope, healing, or help others need. What a tragedy. We so desperately need better influencers, for the sake of others and for the sake of the world.

So here are the questions driving this book: What does make or break our influence in other's lives? What, in me, hinders people from experiencing the good things God wants for them? And what can I do about it? What are the personal barriers I must overcome to cultivate extraordinary influence?

I know influence is a loaded word. Some lean into it, because it resonates with their desire to affect change in the world around them. Others pull back—to them, influence sounds too agenda-driven, too me-focused, even manipulative.

Let me come clean: I've embraced the term "influence" because I think that if you are in relationship, you've got influence, period. I can't see any way around that. And the more people you're connected to, the more influence you have.

Downplay the idea or deny the reality and we'll end up thinking we don't have it when we do, making us less able to address personal shortfalls that are actually hurting others. The question is never "do I have influence?" but rather "what kind of influence am I going to have?" My goal is for all of us to overcome those personal barriers preventing us from being that good influence.

This is a personal question, isn't it? Will I be the kind of person who helps others grow toward God's wholeness in life, or will my influence hinder that growth in others? If you've picked up this book, I'm going to make an assumption: you want to help others grow. You want to be a better influencer. You are willing to take responsibility for barriers in your own life which may be hindering another's growth. You are brave enough and committed enough to look at yourself with sober judgment, identifying influence barriers so that as you grow personally, others can grow exponentially.

This is a book for two kinds of people: those who don't think of themselves as leaders, as well as those who do. As

I've watched people influence others, for good or ill, through intentionality or negligence, even by people who would never claim the title of leader, I've come to embrace a wider definition of leadership. John Maxwell codified the maxim "Leadership is Influence," and I fully agree.

But I also want to flip this around to say: If you've got influence, you're in leadership, be that in small or large ways. It's better to acknowledge it and improve the quality of your influence than to deny it and cause harm. For those of you who are in formal leadership roles, this book will help you grow personally so you can help others even more, whether that be in your organization, church, or home.

Simply put, then, this book will help anyone in relationship. You might be a stay-at-home-parent or a CFO in a large company; you might be a pastor, a politician, or a plumber. You might have kids, work with volunteers, or serve actively in a church. This book was written for you. Every context in which we have relationship, we also have influence, and therefore, leadership. So why not be the best influence we can be?

I've structured this book to include three basic movements.

First, we look at ourselves, examining three critical areas of personal growth. Unless we have integrity, knowledge, and humility, we will short-circuit our ability to help others grow as God intended.

Second, we explore four essential interpersonal qualities we must embody if we are to influence anyone for good: empathy, respect, grace, and love.

And finally, building upon the foundation of personal growth and these indispensable qualities of care, there are three essential postures we must adopt in order to inspire and sustain change long-term: a bigger vision than we can imagine, an unshakeable positivity in what people can become, and the enduring patience to see it through, all of which is grounded in God's ultimate desire. All ten of these areas will either be catalysts for good influence or barriers to it.

These ten principles are grounded in the Christian story. To anyone who does not share my faith conviction, let me say this: this book is relevant and practical to people from any faith position or no faith position at all. I really believe that. These ten barriers to good influence, if applied, will help you become a more significant influence in other's lives, regardless of your agreement with me on foundational rationale. I have rooted my thinking deep in the soil of my Christian faith because I don't know any other way to do it —my following of Jesus shapes my way of seeing the world, just as your faith and philosophy shapes yours. The theological and Biblical examples given in this book provide a coherent framework for my life and actions as an influencer.

However, you may not share my faith perspective and I respect that (and I'm thankful you've read this far). If that's you, would you consider coming along anyway? If you are willing to keep an open mind, I know that you will not only find helpful coaching and personal growth, you will also have a better sense of how an active, thinking Christian makes sense of life. And I truly would love to hear from you about how this helped you become a better influencer.

For those who are from a faith perspective, particularly followers of Jesus, you will also find your understanding stretched in new and uncharted ways, coupled with helpful application and challenge.. Regardless of background or experience, we've all got barriers to overcome. That said, I invite you, the reader, to join this journey with me, open to ways we might all be called to grow and change.

All of us want to grow. All of us want to help others grow, too. My hope is that as we look deeply into ways we might help or hinder growth in others, we will embrace the kind of personal changes in us which will then help others become all they were meant to be.

SECTION ONE

How We Influence Others Depends First On How We Influence Ourselves.

Unless we lead ourselves properly, we cannot influence others well. Compelling influencers are growing in integrity, expanding in knowledge, and deepening in humility, for without these three basic traits, we cannot truly help others.

1

INTEGRITY

Search me, God, and know my heart;
test me and know my anxious thoughts.
See if there is any offensive way in me,
and lead me in the way everlasting.
- Psalm 139:23-24 NIV

The tire swing held promise. Tied to a tree overhanging a steep bank, you could swing in an exhilarating arc over the riverbed below. I could feel the G-force just looking at it.

"Is it safe?" I asked Darcy.

"Sure it is," he replied. (Darcy is always confident about these things.)

I tied up my horse and grabbed the tire. After a few deep breaths, I launched. And it was breathtaking... for about 5 seconds. Just as I reached the end of the arc, right when you pause before whooshing back, the tension gave way. With an unforgettable snap, rope, tire, and Tom went down hard. Halfway down the riverbank, I rolled, flailed, and flopped, with all my 13-year-old grace, and came up standing at the bottom. Lucky. Until I felt a sharp ache in my arm. I could barely move it, and when I did, pain shot sharp.

"Are you okay?" Darcy's head appeared over the bank above.

"I'm okay. Hurt my arm." I could hear him laughing as I scrambled back up the bank. In the end, that little thrill ride only cracked my arm, but I got to wear a cast anyway, that whole, hot summer of 1987.

Worst part of the experience? Five miles back on a very rough horse, every bump reminding me that what appears safe can be deceiving. A rope can look strong yet be rotten. Lack of integrity hurts. Well, at least I took one for the team and got rid of that tire swing. (Actually, what am I saying? I'm sure someone just tied it back up for more summer fun.)

Integrity invokes trust, implying strength of character and trustworthiness, that what is promised will match what is delivered, that good words correlate with proper actions. If you think about big engines or massive structures, you want parts and craftsmanship that ensure quality. When we refer to the structural integrity of a bridge, we mean it is sound and strong, built upon proven engineering principles by qualified construction workers and guaranteed by a professional engineer. The integrity of jet engines means they are fully functioning, well-maintained, and safe for everyone sipping their inflight beverages to Omaha. The integrity of a house indicates its strength and security, both above and beneath the soil, now and into the future.

In life, integrity describes a life built upon sound principles, aligned around values of quality and excellence. As people of integrity, we pursue wholeness and coherency in all our relationships, so that our lives match our words, our ideals, and our faith in God.

This is a book about our influence on others as we help them become more whole and more fully human. But we can't talk about our influence on others without first examining our influence on ourselves, because without a growing personal wholeness, how could we help others toward the same? Human wholeness, after all, touches on the very essence of what it means to be human in the first place.

The goal of a rightly ordered life is an increasing vitality and congruence across all relationships, work, spirituality, ideas, and priorities. Nothing is exempt. Growing in integrity means that the gap between who I am on the outside and who I am on the inside is closing—not closed, necessarily, but closing. Furthermore, it draws us toward God's ultimate goal for all humans—flourishing relationships in every sphere of life.

Integrity is more about direction than perfection. It's more about who we are becoming than a standard we are attaining. In simple terms, integrity means we aim to do what we say, we strive to live what we preach, and we expect the same growth in ourselves that we are attempting to inspire in others. Our life is becoming more coherent.

When we think of becoming healthy influencers, there is a sense in which we do come first. We must lead ourselves where we are hoping others will go. We invite the Holy Spirit's transformation personally long before we try to encourage others in their personal transformation.

What does that mean? Well, first, we need to pay attention to our own influences. Who has shaped us? Who is shaping us? What is forming my ideas? How am I being affected by various ways of thinking, different types of experiences, forms of social media, and diverse kinds of friends?

The more we articulate what influences us, the better we can tend to our influence of others. Unexamined influences, however, foster a lack of self-awareness, which hinders growth. In order to achieve greater influence in the lives of others, we must experience deep, personal transformation.

And so, we start with this question: "Am I growing in integrity?" Our goal for influence is never to simply affect a person's thinking or get their behaviour to conform to a certain standard. Certainly not to our standards. Our goal is to inspire others to make true, lasting changes that will then help others do the same. But unless we cultivate consistent personal growth, we will never influence others effectively. What's more, if we aren't growing, we won't be the kind of people worthy to influence. Who we are and who we are becoming is foundational to our influence. Let's go there first.

Pursuing Personal Integrity

We live in a cynical time. We expect our leaders to lack integrity, though we decry it when we see it. Promising something in order to gain a hearing, but later changing plans and failing to follow through on those promises—this is considered normal. This cynicism plagues not only our politicians, but our parents, our pastors, our bosses, even our BFFs. We assume that others will let us down. Many outside the church believe the church is full of hypocrites, thinking Christians "say one thing and do another."

Is that cynicism justifiable? Well, in some cases obviously it is not—there are true, honest people of utmost integrity all around us. If we get in close, we can see that for ourselves.

But often the cynicism is warranted. Christians do criticize others for certain choices while secretly committing the same sin. Parents make wild promises to get their kids in line, only to back out later. And that lack of integrity is killing influence. Our ability to influence diminishes in direct proportion to our hypocrisy.

Does integrity imply perfection? Must we live impeccable lives, because without absolute consistency all hopes of influencing anyone for good is gone? Not at all. In fact, it's our very definition of integrity that must change. We've got to stop holding up impossible ideals which guarantee failure. Hypocrisy charges are often laid in areas Christians had no right to ever suggest perfection. As a result, we've prevented both Christians and people of no faith or other faiths from being honest about ways we are struggling toward integrity.

Integrity does not equal perfection; that belief is a guaranteed recipe for continued hypocrisy, because no one is perfect. Even a person striving for integrity will inevitably reveal gaps, lapses, mistakes, and sins, as well as changes in thinking and practice, shifts in perspectives and priorities, and extenuating circumstances.

We are dynamic, growing creatures living in a complex, broken world. Christians open themselves wide to disdain when they perpetuate the idea that we must always show the good and never reveal the struggle.

For example, failing to be honest about marriage struggles makes everyone think you've got it all together. Then, when the relationship falters or the union crumbles, people realize all that bluster about a godly marriage had smeared over simmering problems. It is as though we think that any hint of struggle or weakness would hinder people from seeing Jesus, when, in fact, the opposite is true.

Leaders within organizations, churches, and government feel tempted to spin everything positively. The pressure to be right, to never show weakness, to exude confidence and good plans has forced leaders to project a lot more confidence than they should. When they inevitably falter, hypocrisy is the charge. They do this because they think honesty will hurt influence.

The opposite is actually true: if we will be clearer about our desire for integrity, and more honest about the ways we are struggling to achieve it, we will receive more grace from others and, perhaps surprisingly, more influence in their lives. People want to join us in the fight, to journey with us, rather than feel like they must either bow in awe before someone who's already arrived or reject this hypocrite who must be hiding his or her true self.

Integrity is not attaining perfection but growing toward wholeness. Pastor Craig Groeschel loves to repeat the mantra, "People would rather follow a leader who's always real than a leader who's always right." That is true for leaders, yes, and parents, and pastors, and politicians. Let's make it more so.

How do we do this? How do we become more honest about our struggles and our growth? How do we make sure we are pursuing personal integrity before personal influence? We start by getting honest, becoming more open about how we are growing in our self-understanding, how we are wrestling to reorder our own minds and hearts and lives. We admit mistakes and become more transparent about our struggles, whether in our attitudes, our thinking, our choices, our sin, our positions, our theology, or our relationships.

Some of the ways we foster more authenticity as leaders is by rejecting the status of celebrity or guru. Perhaps not many of us will be considered a guru, but what about when others begin to see us as good examples or even authority figures, holding us up as paragons of integrity, as people who *aren't* hypocritical, as men and women who really do live out what they say? And while we can be thankful for that expanding influence, that's a very tippy place to be. We've finally achieved what we've been working toward—a solid platform from which to lead change! But it is at that moment that we are in more danger than ever.

To steward good influence, we must reject celebrity. We must cut down the guru claims by becoming actively transparent, openly candid about ways we are still growing. We need to share personal stories of struggle, even ugly struggles such as pride or independence or laziness. Let people see your own attempts to wrestle with the implications of truth in your own life.

I can tell you how powerful this pull to be "a cut above the rest" really is, to exude a kind of false spirituality that belies true reality. Pastors get this reinforced daily, as people assume you are more holy and more connected to God than they are *because you are a pastor.* That's just not true. (Of course, you already knew that.) I need to continually create space for the Spirit's work in my life, just as all followers of

Jesus do. And I am desperately in need of grace all along the way.

This is where the honest habit of self-examination is crucial. If we are not regularly reflecting (alone and with others) on the ways our lives are not matching our words, then we will never be able to be candid with others about our own growth.

Unless we are doing the hard work of deep integration, we will gravitate toward the messages that confirm what we always wanted—the wonderful status of being authentic without working the practices that lead to true authenticity. Wouldn't it be better to shave down our own reputations in advance, reminding people of who we are and how we are growing, than have their vision of us cut down when our less-than-perfect character shows through?

By being honest, even a bit more self-revealing than we might be comfortable with, we invite people into a journey toward personal integrity themselves. We model the pathway toward integrity, rather than just its destination. We show people how we can, together, move toward greater wholeness. We influence others to grow as we are growing.

Recently, I experienced depression for the first time in my life. I know and love many who struggle with mental illness, but I had a hard time recognizing it in myself. I was shy about naming my own pain, but as time went on, I felt the pull to be more honest about how I was doing.

So, little by little, I started sharing with friends that I was not doing great, that I was feeling really down, that I was looking for a counselor. When I finally began therapy, I told my church about it. Were some put off by this honesty from the pastor preaching from the front? Perhaps, but far more were inspired by it, and I have been supported and loved and encouraged through the process. What's more, it's allowed me to put into practice what I've been preaching for years: that we need to be more open and transparent about mental health struggles. I just didn't know that I'd need to lead that myself.

Integrity is About Our Whole Lives

When we consider personal integrity, we are talking about wholeness of life through the whole of our lives. Integrity arches over everything. I know that's not always been true. There have been people of influence who have integrity in one aspect of their lives while severely lacking it in another.

For example, business owners who demonstrate tremendous integrity in their work and yet fail to pursue wholeness in their home. Professors who demonstrate rigorous standards in their scholarship and yet neglect their spiritual growth.

But we are not interested in integrity by compartments, as though one part of the house (the siding, let's say) is hardy and weather-resistant, whereas we are losing roofing shingles by the day. We must tend to the integrity of the entire house, where each aspect of our lives is moving from disintegration and brokenness toward re-integration and wholeness.

And what is being re-integrated and made whole? The four relationships that make us human. Being fully human is about the flourishing and integration of our relationship with God (spirituality), our relationship with others (marriage, family, friends, community), our relationship with the world (earth, animals, work, art, music, culture) and our relationship with ourselves (mental, physical, emotional, creativity, personal vitality).

These four relationships mutually reinforce each other, and together they form the whole of our human lives. Nothing falls outside of them, and in order to live a fully human life, we cannot neglect any one of them nor keep them isolated from each other.

But I am convinced that we have neglected some or isolated some from others. We have often chosen to emphasize one aspect of our human lives while rudely rejecting another. We've favoured our relationship with God over our care for the poor, a mindset that runs counter to the teaching of Jesus and yet has been perpetuated by Christians at various times. Knowing this is a false dichotomy, Christians are working hard to restore the whole good news of Jesus, who seeks to bring spiritual healing while at the very same time addressing the hurts and injustices in the larger human society.

We have also neglected certain aspects within one of the four areas, for example failing in marriage while fiercely volunteering. Abdicating our responsibility to be in relationship with the rest of God's creation is still too common —even though the very first mandate given to the human images of God in the Bible is to rule, protect, and serve the earth and its inhabitants (Genesis 1-2). And we have long failed to understand the significance of our own internal relationship, the way I think and interact and love my own self, as a fragmented, sinful yet glorious and beloved human being.

Diverse traditions, times, and theologies have tended to favour certain relationships over others, and it is interesting to identify which ones have been favoured or neglected within our own experience. By understanding our inherited biases, we are better able to shore up what has been missing and experience deeper integration.

Pursuing integrity, then, is our commitment to bring greater wholeness to all four relationships and to foster mutual interdependence between them. The goal is for the full integration of our relationship with God, others, the world, and ourselves. Fully attainable in this life? No, but a wonderful journey of discovery and grace along the way, bringing with it the experience of beauty and wholeness and life which acts as a live preview of God's promised new creation.

Dive into any one of these four relational areas and we realize how much healing and grace we need. Who among us is living all four with perfect synchronicity? No one. And that should both humble us and inspire us, because it is in the pursuit of these relationships that we become more human, more whole, more righteous, more of who God created us and calls us to be, as well as able help others experience the same. It's a grace-filled journey, as Jesus walks with us, offering us the grace we need ourselves, and helping us offer that grace to others.

To return to our bridge and jet engine analogy, the integrity of our lives will help people go somewhere they may not have gone otherwise. If our lives can act as a bridge for others, so that our integrity helps them move forward in an area of their lives, then we will have influenced someone toward greater personal and relational flourishing. If we tend to the maintenance of our own engines, we will be able to take people on a journey toward wholeness in a way that helps them process their own journey and experience more integrity themselves.

But the bridge must have integrity. The engines must be maintained. Our integrity matters if we are to influence others in healthy and meaningful ways. This leads us to consider ways we do that as leaders—how do we grow and maintain our integrity?

When we consider our influence, we must embrace a dialectical truth: even though influence is not all about us, it does start with us. When we think of God's whole plan for the world's redemption and recreation, we are tiny players in a very big mix. The little bit of influence we do have, for the short time we have it, reminds us to stay humble and to forgo grandiose delusion.

However, within that plan, we do have influence, and in order to become truly helpful, we must start with ourselves. We must take responsibility for our own relationship with God, our own relationships with others, our own relationships with the rest of God's creation, and in our own inner life. We have no other starting point, even though, at the end of the day, we are not the point!

We need to think practically about how we can foster greater personal integrity, so that we experience more wholeness, beginning with us and radiating throughout all the four relational aspects of human life. Let's explore some postures to help us do exactly that.

Three Postures of Personal Integrity

Confession. Personal integrity is more about our direction than our perfection. We need to get honest about where we are, so we don't just glide over the inconsistencies within our hearts, minds, and lives. Confession is a central posture for Christians, as we acknowledge our own failure and need for God's grace and forgiveness.

But we need more than the confession of sin—we need to adopt confession as a more personal posture within our network of relationships. As we already explored, we need to intentionally confess to ways we are still working toward integrity, as well as ways we are not yet living up to our own hopes and expectations.

Obviously, depending on the depth of the inconsistency or the struggle we are facing, there needs to be wisdom on what is shared and a selectivity with whom we share. But that doesn't change the fact that we shouldn't be hiding from everyone. And the more we are willing to confess appropriately our own inconsistency or struggle, the more we will grow in integrity and the more we will be seen as a person who is growing in integrity.

Perhaps the simplest example can be seen in parenting. My kids see more of the real me than most. They see me when I'm frustrated, when I let my guard down and say something nastier than I would say publicly, when I do something small but inconsistent with my own values. I need to be willing to own up to those failures, inconsistencies, and sins.

To say to my own kids, "I messed up here. I shouldn't have said that. I'm sorry." Does that reduce my integrity in their eyes? No, it raises it—they had already witnessed the inconsistency, and now they see my honesty about my own failure and my willingness to be honest and state what I am aiming for. Integrity is more about direction than perfection.

Continual growth and learning. Another posture critical to our integrity is one of continual growth and learning. Learning is central to self-leadership, charting a course for getting better and taking time every day to work on yourself. How is that connected to integrity? It's in the awareness that there is much we don't know, that we have so much to learn and so many ways we must develop. By taking that seriously, we will be influencers who are always growing, always receiving, always taking in the insights and challenges of others.

A great example within my pastoral vocation would be continual theological growth. There's a temptation to always have a quick and ready answer, to become overconfident in our theological positions and suggest to people that we've got everything settled in our thinking. But that's just not true.

Yes, there are certain theological positions about which Christians are firmly convinced, and the authority of Scripture guards and guides us. But there are also many areas in flux, which are dynamically unfolding, in which we are growing and changing.

My understanding of God and my engagement with Scripture is a live, active, bubbling reality, moving me and provoking me and helping me grow. I am on a course of constant growth as well, and so I must model that dynamic of change and development, even within my own theology.

The truth is, without a learning posture, we won't be very compelling influencers, especially to those younger than us. But demonstrate insatiable curiosity, pursuing a constant course of growth? People will be inspired to learn from you. (More on this in chapter two.)

Humility. The two postures of ready confession and continual learning leads us naturally to a third posture: humility. Humility is so critical to our influence that we will focus a whole chapter on it (chapter 3). For now, let's touch on how significant humility is to integrity.

When people accuse leaders of hypocrisy, it is not because they were expecting perfection. It's because they were hoping for someone real and didn't find it. So, let's get real. As you examine your own life and relationships, be honest about the areas you have noticed neglect and need growth. Have you over emphasized your relationship with people and neglected your relationship with the planet? Confess your own neglect and talk about ways you are addressing that missing area—practices you are changing, books you are reading, or ways you are correcting that imbalance.

My wife and I realized over 15 years ago that we had ignored the connection between God's creation and the other three relational areas (God, ourselves, and others). We experienced this disconnection as a growing sense of unease, a feeling that somehow our lives lacked integrity.

And so, very slowly, God led us on a journey of personal and life change. We initiated a more earth-careful discipleship, little step by little step and faltering along the way. We asked questions. We read some books. We started growing food. We sought solace in creation. Frankly, we weren't very good at it.

Eventually, we bought a small farm on which to raise our two sons, not as a rejection of the city (we love the city!) but as an expression of our ongoing discipleship of Jesus and our desire to integrate our neglected relationship with creation into our relationship with God, each other, and ourselves.

And how has that gone? It's been hard. It's expensive. And we only get it right some of the time. There's nothing romantic about it. And there are days we just want to quit (and maybe we will at some point). But for now, we venture forward, daily pursuing integrity in this area as we feel God has led us, dimly aware of how much we are missing the mark and yet soldiering on.

And we hope that our attempts to live within the four fundamental relationships God set up, however falteringly, will help others ask themselves questions about how they, in their own context, are also pursuing greater integrity.

Having humility on this path of growth, all the while confessing our failures to live it all out perfectly, helps us grow. We are able to receive God's grace for the ways we fail and offer grace to others around us. And, as we will see, humility will, in the end, create greater influence than any overconfident bravado, bravado which is not only false, but also discourages others from joining the stumbling journey forward.

So, how can we foster integrity? The three postures of confession, learning, and humility lead us to *do* certain things, and the cultivation of particular habits will in turn create more awareness of our need for growth and more willingness to confess that need in humility. They are mutually reinforcing.

When we think of these practices, it's as though we are learning to use common tools for building a house, tools which are not in and of themselves the point but help us grow toward our goal of greater integrity. The fact is, we naturally drift toward diffusion, not integrity.

We need intention and intention needs tools. I want to suggest five practices that will help build your integrity, tools that must be employed in a person's life on a regular basis.

Five Practices for Building Integrity

Daily Reading. The first integrity-building practice is our daily reading. In order to experience personal growth and transformation, we must commit to a habit of daily, intentional reading. I'm not talking about all of us becoming academics. What we read can vary, but I believe that some of it must touch on personal and spiritual transformation if it is to be helpful for our integration.

For followers of Jesus, the daily reading of the Bible is essential to nurturing the four basic relationships: God, others, creation and our own selves. Putting God's word in my heart and life aids my ongoing transformation "by the renewing of my mind" (Rom 12:2).

In order to keep consistent, I follow some kind of a daily reading plan. I can't leave it all up to whim or I'll wander off. I've found the YouVersion Bible App, with its many plans, to be incredibly helpful, but any paper plan works, too.

In addition to Scripture, spiritual reading is also important, which is extra reading that supports, enhances, and corrects my relationship with God, and thus shapes all my other relationships, too. These resources may include one of the Christian classics, a current devotional book, or a collection of poetry.

And then, if possible, our reading can expand from there to enhance our growth in multiple areas. I believe that taking in other people's stories through biography or autobiography, watching them fail, witnessing both their tragedies and their triumphs—all help us grow toward integrity.

Reading specifically designed to develop an area of need

(leadership, personal health, listening, parenting, etc.) is also critical. Identifying a few of those key areas and then setting some modest reading goals (like a book a month, where each month covers a specific area), will go a long way toward helping us with personal integration.

Daily reading is critical to building personal integrity. And a regular diet of intentional reading, even taken in small portions, will have great effect. A typical day might include, for example, 15 minutes of Scripture reading, followed by a short reading from a classic or a poem in the morning. Later in the day, you may take in a bit more in your chosen "book-of-the-month." Freely adjust the times to fit you, spanned over a day, a week, or a month. It's far better to do a little reading, which adds up over the long haul, than to set your expectations too high and never read anything at all.

One helpful way to read more is to listen while on the move. Thankfully, audiobooks and Bible apps have made our books and Bibles easily accessible, which is great particularly for auditory learners. Feel free to mix it up. Listen to your Bible reading while on a walk, work through a personal growth book on the treadmill or while driving to work. Use the gift of technology to enhance your own growth, wherever you are.

Podcasts. The subject of audio moves us to my second integrity-building practice: listening to podcasts. I am a podcast fan because I've experienced so much growth through them. There's something great about filling in the cracks of my driveway or going for a walk while learning from others across the country and around the world. Hearing interviews, receiving insight, learning new skills across a broad range of interests makes us better.

I like how podcasts usually range from 20 minutes to an hour (with some notable exceptions) and how they naturally complement our personal growth. You don't have to listen all the time (silence is important, too), but having some regular podcast conversations are critical to our integration. Podcasts can fit into areas we've already mentioned, such as spirituality, leadership, and biography, but they can also fill in many other areas of interest or learning, from cooking or marketing or history to philosophy or parenting. I'd suggest finding a few that really fit and then subscribing to receive their latest downloads.

Mentors. However, integrity-building tools would be very isolating and sad if they were only reading and listening! That's why our third practice is finding a mentor or guide. We need people in the flesh, helping us sift through the growth happening within our own lives. Finding a mentor, a spiritual director, a counselor, or a spiritual friend helps us process our learning, including our successes and our failures, with honesty.

Too many of us don't have anyone with whom we are transparent and authentic. As a result, we experience disintegration, with pieces and experiences and failures and insights all rattling around without coherence or pattern. In a relationship with an experienced guide, we can pull these pieces out of the mix, examine them thoughtfully, honestly, and candidly, and then slowly and prayerfully begin putting them back together in a more integrated way.

Finding someone to walk with us can be difficult. We can face internal resistance to the very idea. For years, I resisted this practice. I even found a spiritual director once, and then started avoiding him and stalling out and putting him off—for close to two years! Thankfully another friend pushed me to return, and I was glad I did.

As someone who has both experienced the tremendous help of a guide (in my case, a spiritual director *and* a counsellor), as well as the deep hesitancy to finding that guide, I can tell you that it is worth it. Push through your hesitations. Take the step. Make the call. Finding a mentor, hiring a counselor, engaging a spiritual director, or initiating an intentional spiritual friendship for the purpose of confidential, shared conversations is a critical tool for our pursuit of integrity.

Written Self-Examination. Which bring us to practice number four: self-examination through journaling. All this reading, listening, and sharing helps us hear and ask good questions. We are more able to recognize areas within our hearts, minds, and lives that are not adding up. Places where the gaps are not closing and might even be growing wider.

Our lack of self-awareness leads to less integrity and diminishes our influence. Because of the space we've created to receive more insight and truth in our lives, we are now able to reflect more honestly and critically on our lives. And this is where we delve down into that fourth, fundamental relationship—our relationship with our internal selves—seeking God's healing and wholeness within the deepest places of our personhood.

How we capture that self-examination can vary, but journaling has been a very helpful tool to many people, and so I recommend it to you. It is remarkable how illuminating it has been to write out my processing, my questions, my wonderings and then see what I've written, both in the moment and (more powerfully) through the patterns revealed over a period of time.

Writing brings clarity in ways that an unwritten reflection simply cannot. We aren't able to hold all our thoughts and musings together in ways that lead to helpful self-examination. Not everyone finds regular journaling easy, but those who have swear by it.

For years, my journaling was intermittent—I'd find it useful on silent retreats or in moments of quiet but barely journal on regular days. Only recently has it become more daily for me. But regardless of frequency, building regular times of self-examination into our lives is critical to our integrity. Whether it is on a day retreat at a local monastery or an hour a month in a coffee shop, take time to stop, examine, and capture it in writing.

Solitude and Silence. Our fifth practice for building integrity is planned solitude and silence. Full confession: I'm a noise guy. I love the buzz of a coffee shop. I pump music on my speakers at home and podcasts while I'm driving. It can drive my wife nuts! And yet, I, too, am convinced we need silence in our lives.

Some of us naturally crave silence, while others of us will need to schedule it in. But we all need time to be quiet, perhaps for a few moments every day, but also for longer periods of time. We can't always be taking in, taking in, taking in—we must also rest, sit, and be still.

The practice of daily meditation has been helpful for many across many traditions—it's almost impossible without silence and solitude. I have come to deeply appreciate silent retreats when I go away and hear nothing more than the wind and the birds and the stillness for hours and sometimes days at a time.

Silence centers us and helps us to attend more fully to the voices we hear in our daily lives. Think that's impossible? Talk to a friend and see how you can support each other in that, even to get away for a few hours a month. I know you can.

These five tools help us examine, repair, and strengthen our integrity. On a house, we can deal with problems as we identify them, or cover them over so no one sees. But covering over a problem or pretending it doesn't exist doesn't solve anything, does it?

When we bought our old house, it had a raised subfloor built in the basement. How nice, we thought—it keeps our toes insulated from the cold concrete below. That is, until we discovered months later that the subfloor had been built to deal with a leaky basement. When the annual spring rains came, so did the annual basement flood. So—get this—instead of dealing with the source of the problem, the former owners built a sub-floor to cover over a recurring symptom. The rains came, and the floods rose, but no matter—they were now walking three inches above the high-water line! Well, that might have worked for a few years, but as you can imagine, a whole lot was going on out of sight and mind. When I removed the floor, so much of it was rotten that I had to scrape it out with a shovel.

Our lives are like houses. We can have hidden areas, wasting away beyond our sight. In order to have influence we must have the courage to pull up the floorboards and look to the integrity of our foundations. All these tools will help us to do just that: tend to the parts of our lives often hidden beneath soil and wood, addressing aspects that, if left unexamined and unrepaired, will result in the disintegration of the very relationships that matter most.

How Our Integrity Helps or Hinders Our Influence

Growing our integrity is foundational to enhancing our influence. Knowing how important it is to build our foundation, to regularly and faithfully tend to our personal integrity and growth, let's now explore ways integrity helps or lack of integrity hinders our influence in other's lives.

As I've been noting all along, we live and influence within our four fundamental relationships with God, others, the world, and ourselves. Much of our personal growth and learning takes place in that personal interaction between us and God, as well as in dynamic conversation with our own inner selves. Yes, within the context of creation, and, yes with the help from other people such as authors and teachers and mentors (though they act more as influences upon us than areas we influence).

Where influence really happens—and such is the force of this book—is in the other two relational areas—the people in our lives and the world in which we all live. And our ability to provide good, wise, and healthy influence in those two areas will be directly proportional to our personal integrity.

How we act. When we consider our influence in the lives of other people and within God's world, the first thing to explore is how we live, in particular how we act. We must ask ourselves the fundamental question to measure our own integrity: Do our actions match what we say we believe? If they do, then we are considered people of increasing integrity, and our influence is more helpful. If they don't, then we are viewed as people of less integrity and our influence can hurt.

How we live, then, is a key way we influence others.

When I think of my own life, I know how important modelling is, both in my actions and in my speech. As I already mentioned, throughout the first decade of the new millennium, my wife and I became increasingly convinced that we were missing something in our Christian discipleship—like an ache in the stomach, we longed for a more God-honoring relationship with God's good earth.

In terms of the four relationships, we felt that while the other three were growing in our lives, this one was almost non-existent. And so, after many prayerful baby steps we took one, giant leap: we purchased a small farm and moved to the Creston Valley of British Columbia. And we did that as a journey toward greater personal integrity, attempting to shore up a flagging relationship and correct a gross imbalance within our four relationships.

With no suggestion that anyone should do the same thing (quite honestly, they probably shouldn't!), we knew that we needed to respond to God's call to live more faithfully as stewards of God's creation, and we felt this was the way we needed to do it. Others must do it in other ways, within their own context of city, suburb, strata, or slum. Our choice was not inherently better and could be criticized as a flight from much needed city ministry. For us, it was the step we needed to take to be more faithful to God's call on us.

However, we also knew that this had to be a move toward integrity for us, not simply to help others. The motivation had to be personal integrity before God, not personal influence toward others. In other words, we couldn't just move to a farm, throw a few seeds in the ground, hatch a few chicks out, and then immediately begin talking about earth care and local food and stewardship as though we now had some kind of authority to influence others.

There was a temptation to do so, and yet we couldn't speak about this kind of life without living it first—and living it for a while. We needed to experience this kind of integration before speaking about it, and that has been so, so important.

First, we needed to deeply integrate these things into our personal lives—we couldn't just be caring for God's earth in order to be an example or try to teach something—no, it needed to be real.

But also—and this is so critical—by doing it for a while, all the romanticism and idealism that is so unhelpful to true and lasting influence was drained out of our experience. Trying to restore this old farm has tempered us, showing us how difficult it really is to live earth-carefully, how expensive it is, how time-consuming, how utterly exhausting.

And what has happened? Well, living in this way is now, after some years, allowing us to share, much more modestly, from a place of authenticity. We don't want to hold ourselves up as models. We don't suggest a whole lot of solutions. We aren't nearly as critical of others as we might once have been. We only want to help others live within their own contexts faithfully, wherever they are.

But—and this is important—I do think the integrity of our actions in life have deepened our ability to influence others, fostering meaningful conversations with other people, especially Christians, about how loving God and loving others finds concrete, practical expression in how we steward God's good earth.

Our actions do speak louder than our words, but our words are also important, so long as they mesh with our reality. Integrity doesn't mean we can only speak when our lives have fully matched our ideals.

Not only will that never happen, but we will fall into the trap of perfectionism, which discourages others from growing and opens ourselves up to charges of hypocrisy yet again. No, our words must match the reality of our own journey, that even as we hold up ideals we are advancing, we are honest and transparent about the ways we are struggling toward that ideal.

Perhaps what helps us most with that is a re-examination of our own priorities, based on how we live and speak. Do our priorities in life, indicated by our calendars and budgets, reflect our larger convictions? For example, we say we want to see young people mentored toward maturity in Christ and commitment to his mission, but do we commit time and finances to creating and sustaining mentoring programs? Do we get training and make ourselves available as ready mentors? We say that strengthening our marriages is important within society and as a church, but are we booking time away with our own spouse? Are we reading books on marriage? Are we encouraging habits that enhance marriage among our friends and then helping each other to practice them? It is only when our actions and our priorities align with our convictions that our influence will grow.

How we think. But our actions come from somewhere, don't they? Yes, and that's why our pursuit of integrity must extend beyond our actions to the very ways that we think. Through personal growth and self-examination, as well as in active practice of the things we deem important, we come closer to understanding our own convictions.

Why do I even think that? What is at the foundation of

my conviction? Does my thinking even match reality, or have I harboured lies within my own mind? In order to influence others, we must influence the way they think, not through manipulative mind-control, but by shifting perspective, offering insight, and encouraging honesty.

But in order to do that, we must pursue integration within our own thinking. Is my conviction grounded in truth—the truth of God's Word, the practice of good theology, the best of science, and the application of godly wisdom? Am I open to receiving instruction, input, and feedback from others? Or, when I dig into it, is my thinking missing key elements?

I often see (within myself and others) underdeveloped thinking presented with such confidence that it can seem, for the moment, very compelling. That is, until more facts come to light, more reflection is done, or more voices are added to the mix, exposing the error and overturning the faulty thinking.

People become rightfully suspicious of others whose faulty thinking is found out after the fact, by the facts. If we are to influence another's thinking, we need increasing integrity in our own, which we will explore more in the next chapter on knowledge.

Integrity is critical to influence. But at the end of the day, not everyone will find our integrity compelling. In fact, no matter how much personal integrity we do have, there will be those less open to our influence for a variety of reasons. Perhaps they oppose our ideas at a fundamental level, or they are inherently suspicious that we have some hidden agenda. Or maybe we can provide some influence in one area (for example, in how we engage debate with humility and grace) but are not able to influence in another area (like making a certain organizational change).

Some will see our pursuit of integrity as prudish or too intense. Others might find that our pursuit of integrity challenges them to address areas of their lives where they are profoundly dis-integrated. Through no intention or attitude of our own, they will respond cynically, questioning our intentions even when we feel we have been clear, humble, and honest. And of course, there are others, frankly, who just won't care.

Whatever the case, when we face people who are resistant to our help or influence, we must remember that we pursue integrity because it's right and holy and good, not because it's simply an effective tool for influencing others. The God who made us whole and saw us break wants to see us whole again.

Integrity is about being a person that is growing and developing in the four relationships which makes us human, honest about our failures and striving to become more whole. While integrity has practical effect, we don't embrace it as something to use only when handy, like a tool picked up or discarded depending on the job at hand.

Integrity is who we are—it's about embracing our full identity as human images of God. As such, it will affect all our relationships, and therefore the level of our influence. But it's not optional. If the only reason we pursue integrity is to help others change, then it won't last. If integrity is just a show, just a tool, people will see through that and your influence will diminish.

Integrity, at its core, is all about your own personal growth. It's about your self-leadership. And if you are leading yourself well, then you will be far more able to lead others well. Who I am personally greatly affects who I am able to influence, over the long term.

When we pursue integrity through postures of confession, growth, and humility, actively practicing habits which lead us toward wholeness in our relationships, actions, and thinking, we will experience significant growth. And that growth, coupled with the following nine characteristics of growing influencers, will lead to transformation in our families, our churches, our communities, and our world.

Reflection Questions

- How does defining integrity as direction rather than perfection affect the way you pursue integrity?
- What is the interconnection between vulnerability and integrity?
- When you consider our four basic relationships (with God, others, creation, and our own inner selves), which relationship in your life has been most neglected and how will you address that?
- Which of the three integrity-building postures (confession, learning, and humility) struck you as your greatest challenge?
- How will you incorporate key integrity-building practices into your life over the next 30 days?

2

KNOWLEDGE

The fear of the LORD is the beginning of knowledge,
but fools despise wisdom and instruction.
- Proverbs 1:7 NIV

Few things are less convincing than an ill-formed thought. If we want to help others grow and change, we have to know what we are talking about. As we have witnessed in the political arena and in conversations on social media, we live in a time when our rhetoric seems less dependent upon truth and more reliant upon opinion. We seem to be championing the motto, "Yell louder, and they'll be convinced."

We need to do better; we need to model more effective ways of engaging divisive and polarizing positions. When something we believe is true is attacked, we need to remain confident in the power of the truth, even if we aren't entirely sure what that truth is sometimes. And when we do believe that our position represents the truth or the best position available, we must not stoop, in the heat of the moment, to means and methods beneath personal integrity.

Name calling and foul bluster might get cheers from the home team, but it kills any further influence we might have had with others who don't yet agree with us. Viewed through the lens of influence, we can take a more pragmatic approach.

What words or behaviors will enhance influence rather than deepen disagreement? How can my understanding grow so that I am able to represent the sides of this debate accurately and then present the best position available? Because without knowledge, influence wanes and we are left with empty, ignorant rhetoric.

The Oxford Dictionary's Word of the Year for 2016 was "post-truth," defined as an adjective "relating to or denoting circumstances in which objective facts are less influential in shaping public opinion than appeals to emotion and personal belief." Had any "post-truth" conversations lately?

In a time when knowledge and truth seem to matter less, both sides within polarized debates seem eager to accuse each other of playing fast and loose with the real facts. Fake news, anyone? But in a time when facts seem less important than they once did, I want to argue that they are more critical than ever.

Knowledge grows influence. We can see that all around us. People who know something well can help others more. So, to be truly influential, we must be always learning, always receptive to thought, insight, opinion, and expertise, knowing that much of our influence extends only as far as our knowledge.

Now you might be thinking: *if that were true, then how are so many people being influenced by others who don't seem to know what they are talking about?* But truth will win in the end. Yes, people do follow ill-informed leaders. People do align themselves with positions that protect their interests, even if they aren't coherent or true. Some are simply attracted to confidence, to surety, to leaders who boldly represent what they feel or believe, even if they are not logically strong positions. In a muddled world, people long to make sense of their lives; when clarity is offered (even if it's false), it's often gobbled up.

Being committed to the truth means being unwilling to advocate for change for wrong reasons, being unwilling to exercise influence that is more rhetoric than truth and refusing to appeal to greed and fear rather than truth, beauty, and goodness. In other words, it flows from the personal integrity we already discussed.

Humans Are Called to Know and Grow

To become growing influencers, we must first be committed to truth. We must be convinced that there is truth, and that truth, though often mysterious and elusive to us, is at least partially available and potentially attainable. We must be people who love the truth, pursue the truth, and are willing to submit our own lives to the truth.

One of our earliest biblical Proverbs roots our starting point for knowledge in the fear of God. The "fear of the Lord" can evoke a groveling image and be easily misheard—culturally, we don't use the word "fear" in a positive way anymore. But fearing the Lord is not about cowering in terror but bowing in reverence.

Biblically speaking, fear is about our reverence, awe,

trust, and submission to a good God, a gracious King, a loving Saviour. By fearing God, we acknowledge the one who is the source of all truth. Fear is not about cringing before a capricious God or trembling before an exacting deity.

When the Proverbs link the beginnings of our knowledge with the fear of God, the very foundations of knowledge are being unveiled to us. God—the creator and sustainer of the universe, the one who revealed himself through his creation of the good earth and his human images, the one who showed his character through his rescuing love of his people—is the source of all truth and wisdom and insight. There is nothing—never has been anything, never will be something—about which God does not have intimate knowledge, exceeding ours by a googolplex.

And yet the human calling to know and grow is affirmed in Scripture. Not only is the *adam* (or dirtling, if you will) given the responsibility as the first classification biologist in Genesis 2, the human pursuit of knowledge and understanding is an expression of our image-of-God selves. Christians believe that God made the world, and that all creation somehow points to him. We have been able to study the heavens and the earth, the creeping things and the oceans, growing in knowledge springing from our reverent fear of the God who made it all and called it good.

We agree that "The heart of the discerning acquires knowledge, for the ears of the wise seek it out" (Proverbs 18:15 NIV). The wise *seek it out.* We love the truth, and we are in pursuit of it. And that pursuit is rooted in our fear of the Lord and our reverence for the source of all truth.

Even as we read or study or listen or research, we can

pray with the Psalmist, "Teach me knowledge and good judgment, for I trust your commands" (Psalm 119:66 NIV). That gets us closer to the beginnings of wisdom and knowledge—we trust in God's commands.

Perhaps one of the most famous places this all comes together is in Psalm 19. Past readers pointed out how Psalm 19 neatly discerns God's revelation to us through his "two books"—the created world and the inspired Scripture. The Psalm begins with night sky glory: "The heavens proclaim the glory of God. The skies display his craftsmanship" (Psalm 19:1 NLT).

The poem continues for the first six verses, casting a vision of how all creation points to its Creator. The "book" of creation tells a story of its author.

But then Psalm 19 continues, seamlessly, to wax rapturous about the God's written book. Sweeter than honey and more precious than gold, we are enticed by its power to revive and reveal and reward. As we consider knowledge, we read that "The decrees of the Lord are trustworthy, making wise the simple" (Psalm 19:7b NLT).

And that "The commands of the Lord are clear, giving insight for living" (Psalm 19:8b NLT).

Many scientists in history were devout Christians who took great encouragement from this compelling idea that God had written two books and that his character and power could be traced across both the scope of the skies and the papyrus of the page. You will find good historians arguing that this conviction—that God made a good, coherent world that both works practically and reveals God's glory—ignited the scientific revolution from the sixteenth century onwards.

Truth is woven into the warp and woof of our Father's

world, a world which follows rules, principles, axioms, facts, cycles and seasons, even if they are often elusive and difficult to discern. This is what makes science so powerful—our universe has consistency, working in ways that can be observed, doing things we've come to expect, even when it often surprises us with the unexpected.

However, God didn't stop revelation at sky or script. God definitively revealed himself through Jesus Christ. Invoking the Genesis story, John's Gospel begins with "In the beginning was the Word, and the Word was with God, and the Word was God. He was with God in the beginning. Through him all things were made; without him nothing was made that has been made" (John 1:1-3 NIV).

And that Word, which was there in the beginning, with God and was God himself, that Word through whom the first book of revelation was penned and the second book of revelation points, he took the final step of revelation by becoming one of his own creation. "The Word became flesh and made his dwelling among us. We have seen his glory, the glory of the one and only Son, who came from the Father, full of grace and truth" (John 1:14 NIV).

This Word, who is Jesus, made the invisible God visible, for though "No one has ever seen God... the one and only Son, who is himself God and is in closest relationship with the Father, has made him known" (John 1:18 NIV).

This is a culmination in revelation, as the letter to the Hebrews states, "In the past God spoke to our ancestors through the prophets at many times and in various ways, but in these last days he has spoken to us by his Son, whom he appointed heir of all things, and through whom also he made the universe" (Hebrews 1:1-2 NIV).

The Father, who was somewhat "knowable" through

creation, who revealed himself even more clearly in the election, rescue, and formation of his people Israel, made himself fully known in history through the incarnation of his Son, Jesus.

Jesus, who is the Way, the Truth, and the Life (John 14:6), puts to rest that old question about whether truth is absolute or relative. Truth, as we come to see, is actually "a relative," a person, a human being, One with whom we can have a relationship, absolutely.

As the Apostle Paul captured it, it is Jesus "Christ" who "is the visible image of the invisible God."

> *He existed before anything was created and is supreme over all creation, for through him God created everything in the heavenly realms and on earth.*
>
> *He made the things we can see and the things we can't see—such as thrones, kingdoms, rulers, and authorities in the unseen world.*
>
> *Everything was created through him and for him.*
>
> *He existed before anything else, and he holds all creation together* (Colossians 1:15-17 NLT).

Because Jesus is the Truth through which the world was made, because he reigns over all creation, then the world he made follows suit—it reveals his nature as one who is true. To be people committed to the truth means that we are convinced that truth exists, truth is real, that we do not live in a world ruled by shifting shadows and power grabs where "might makes right."

Because truth is real, then we are subject to it—we can't just make stuff up, fudge over inconsistencies, or fabricate confidence in the hopes that no one will ever find out we don't actually know what's going on. Better to be confident that there is truth, even when we aren't sure what it is than to act as though we know and be found out liars. Or worse yet, be found out by people who have trusted themselves to our guidance.

What is the net effect of all this? As followers of Jesus, we believe that truth really exists, woven into our world, revealed in Scripture, and ultimately expressed in Jesus. This clarity holds us steady—we may not know all truth, but we do know truth is real and present. And so, as people committed to truth and yet not in full possession of it, we can only make an impact if we are learning.

To help people grow and change in a certain area of thinking or practice (say, earth care or apologetics), you must commit yourself to becoming more knowledgeable. If an idea is worth promoting or a cause is worth championing, if something is burning inside you that must come out, then grow your knowledge.

In more personal circles, our ability to present an issue clearly, acknowledging what's at stake and understanding the factors involved, will lead to more effective results. And if we can do that in ways that do not elicit defensiveness in others who hold different positions, then we might even see movement in what they believe.

One area where this is crucial for Christians is in the area of sharing personal faith. If a friend asks you over lunch why you think Jesus was such a big deal, are you able to respond in a way that is both knowledgeable and appropriate? Or will you blunder around and say something confusing? And I'm not just talking about nerves—we all can stammer and fritz out under pressure. Nor am I talking about having every answer—being honest about what you don't know is important.

What I'm wondering about, Jesus-follower, is if you know enough to present a coherent response. Not a scholarly lecture. Not a long, detailed answer. But a meaningful one, a compelling one, one that would intrigue someone to ask more questions. Because when you're put on the spot about your faith in Jesus—one of the most important aspects of your life—and you haven't taken it seriously enough to know what you are talking about, then how impactful will you be?

Peter charged us to "Always be prepared to give an answer to everyone who asks you to give the reason for the hope that you have" (1 Peter 3:15 NIV). For any Christian, knowing what you believe and why you believe it is essential to having an effect on someone else's faith journey. Knowledge influences.

But it doesn't need to be something nearly so significant. We can't inspire others towards more healthy eating patterns if we're only parroting what we've heard someone else say. Unless we learn for ourselves, our own ignorance will be revealed and our influence diminished. Apply that to any area you like, from politics to parenting to prayer. The more we take truth seriously, the more potential influence we will have.

Influencing through knowledge also involves admitting when we don't know what we are talking about. None of what I'm saying is meant to suggest that we become walking, talking heads, encyclopedic and overwhelming in every conversation, especially if it touches on our pet topic. Don't be that guy.

We will also *not* know many things, and rather than blustering and faking it, we should clearly say "I don't really know much about that" and then either commit to find out more or help this person find what they are looking for. Because in truth, we can't and don't know everything—we don't have to—but we can help others connect with those who do, and that can be just as influential as knowing it yourself.

There are few realizations less disappointing than finding out the guy who's been going on for fifteen minutes about a subject you find intriguing doesn't really know what he's talking about. Why did he do that? Better to own up to your ignorance, and then work on a strategy for finding out more.

In our personal relationships, we cannot know everything that will come up, and though we may be tempted to represent ourselves as knowledgeable, it's far better to admit our lack. Part of having integrity is being honest about the extent and limits of our knowledge. But we can continue to influence others in the way we go about admitting our ignorance and pursuing understanding—that kind of modeling is much needed today.

As I already mentioned, we also influence others by helping them find out where they can get the information or learning they need. In my mentoring relationships, I try to discover where someone's interest lies and what would help them grow. Often, as you can imagine, it is in areas I am not very knowledgeable. That's okay. I can show curiosity, interest, and openness, which has wonderful effect.

One tactic is to learn together. To support one young leader wrestling with science and faith questions, we read several books together and discussed them. I was able to put her in touch with experts in a field of her interest, and then learn along with her through reading and conversation. This can be done in a variety of ways, from books to podcasts to conferences, TED talks and YouTube. Learning together is powerfully influential, because being part of the learning conversation is to be part of someone's growth.

Our influence doesn't just stop there, however. We can also act as connectors to those who do know more, who really are experts. In a way, that's what we do by helping others find particular information, but we can also make personal connections. You see, though we may hit our own capacity for learning along with someone else and not be able to go much further, we might know someone who can. We are able to introduce people to others who can mentor them, and that in itself, is tremendously influential.

My life has been changed by these kinds of introductions, and I want to do that for others. Rather than leaving someone to randomly search the internet for someone to help them (and people will do that anyway—more power to them), we intentionally connect them to someone with integrity and knowledge. We connect that young entrepreneur to an experienced business owner. We help that child pursue their dreams as a graphic artist by helping them find the right mentor. What we know is important, yes, but who we know when there's stuff we don't know? That can be just as significant.

How to Cultivate Knowledge: A Set of Shaping Statements

Okay, so if growing in knowledge is paramount to influence, how do we cultivate knowledge in our own lives? In chapter one, I outlined some regular practices for building integrity. Now I'd like to expand upon that, suggesting a pathway for growing in knowledge, applicable to any subject or purpose. The best way to mark out this pathway is through a series of personal statements which underscore who we are and shape our pursuit.

First, I am a learner. We must take primary responsibility for our learning, embracing that identity as we read and watch and listen, widely and well. To be influential, we must commit ourselves to overcoming our own ignorance, even ignorance about which we might be ignorant. And we do that by the deliberate expansion of our own minds and experience.

We read history and biography. We learn about culture and philosophy. We watch movies and listen to lectures. We join study groups. We read poetry and novels. We travel, we stop, we get out of the car. We meet new people, right in our hometown. We observe the natural world, and soak in the intricacies and delights of creation. We intentionally take in speakers and authors and adventures and insights we wouldn't naturally receive. We use discernment, yes, but less from personal preference and more by solid recommendations.

When I want to expand my knowledge in a certain area, I go to others who are in that field and glean direction from them. Duff provided me much needed resources around the tragic Canadian residential school system. Valerie helped me figure out how to get this book out to you. Alan is only a call away when I'm stuck on something in my work for the church. A well-researched book will often have bibliographies or suggestions for further reading. But whatever it is and however we do it, we are learners. We are responsible to grow in our own understanding, without which we cannot influence to our fullest potential.

Second, I am curious. Hand in hand with the first, we become cultivators of curiosity. We look at the world with a big question mark hovering above us, wondering as we're wandering each and every day. And this takes work. Some of us are naturally curious, but many of us have lost that child-like trait and need to regain it. How do you grow your own curiosity? Here are a few strategies.

1. Keep asking questions. Why does it work that way? Why this and not that? Where did that come from? Why do I think that? Be more apt to ask a question than share a thought. Observe and ask probing questions. Show more interest in what others are doing than what you are doing. Become a journalist in your own community.

2. Get others talking. Encourage people to share their latest interests. There is nothing more inspiring than hearing someone share their passion, whether that be the training of therapy dogs, the making of banjos, or the history of apples. Master the art of asking leading questions to get people, often the shy and quiet among us, to open up about their projects or passions. And then watch out!

3. Watch documentaries on unfamiliar subjects. You'll be amazed at how your own curiosity is cultivated when you watch someone else following theirs! One of the amazing benefits of your local library, YouTube, or Netflix is the readily accessible, stunningly crafted documentaries designed to expand our understanding, passion, and action.

4. Read books that foster curiosity. Better yet, stories where the author or the characters are themselves following a path of inquiry. *Pilgrim at Tinker Creek* by Annie Dillard was a wonder-changer for me, as I witnessed the travels of her own curious mind and questing heart. I've never been the same.

5. *Put yourself in contexts of wonder and creativity.* Deliberately soak in them. The beauty and wonder of God's creation are great places for that, from your backyard to a mountain trail. But you can also tour art galleries, enjoy aquariums, and drink in local music venues.

Third, I follow others. Particularly I follow people who know more than I do. Whether it's in one of the areas you've identified for deep learning or a broader subject area, don't try to be the smartest person in the room. Get in close with people who are smarter or further along than you and learn from them. This could be a local knowledge expert or a writer, podcaster or YouTuber. But make it a practice to follow people who will lead you to deeper knowledge.

Fourth, I am focused. We need to identify key areas that we want to become more adept in. As we've already said, though we can and should touch on broad areas in our learning, we cannot know everything. I recommend listening widely and then identifying a few areas in which to dive deep. But there are so many possibilities. How can I narrow my focus? By running through a few of the following questions:

1. *Is there a subject that keeps resurfacing for me?* Perhaps it is healthy eating, or maybe it is prayer. Look for common threads, patterns, repeating themes.

2. *What conversations make me mad?* This could be face-to-face conversations or online interactions. It could be a larger cultural agitation, or a dinner table spat. When you find yourself getting hot about something, take a cue! Could that be an area you need to expand upon?

3. *What is an area that, if I knew more, I would be more helpful to others?* We often find ourselves in conversations with people we love who are struggling, and often feel very inadequate to help. And don't get me wrong—we don't always need to be experts in those listening moments. What our friends usually need is someone to hear them, to walk with them, and pray with them. But there might be something that you realize would help address the problem, be it an ongoing faith struggle or a parenting need or a health concern. More than a few times, I've dug into an area for the sake of someone else. By learning more, we become more helpful.

4. *What is a subject that you should know more about?* We all have them. I know within my work as a pastor, there have been areas of theology and Biblical study that I've stumbled onto that I know I should have known more about. I took that as a cue to buy some books, consult some experts, and grow in my own understanding so that I am, hopefully, more equipped to help people when questions rise. Recently, I was faced with a choice for a final project in a theology class I was taking for ordination. So, rather than going with something more benign, I took the opportunity to sink my teeth into a subject I'd been avoiding for a few years now (yes, pastors do that.) We are all busy, so areas can be neglected. What is one weak area for you? Perhaps it's even a topic on which others think you are more informed than you are, where you are even expected to be more versed than is actually true?

5. *And what are you passionate about?* Is it vegetable gardening? Fermentation? YouTube? Conservation? Finances? Then go for it. Dive deep. You may already know a lot about this area but let me encourage you. In an area of

passion, you have incomparable opportunity. With dedication over time, intentional study could grow you to be one of the most well-informed and influential people in that field. Don't think so? It has been said that by reading for an hour a day in your chosen field, you could be a leading, international expert in seven years. I'm not sure how that's measured, or if being an international expert is a helpful goal, but what I do know is that focused learning in an area of passion will propel you toward greater influence.

6. And now, step back and observe. Even as you combed through these questions, were there common themes? Is there something that shows up more than once? More than twice? Is there a subject that you felt your heart start racing just thinking about it, or took you back to a recent conversation you had with a friend? Identify one or two key areas for your focus and begin learning more about those areas today.

Fifth, I am committed. Don't leave important learning to chance or whim. Create an intentional learning plan! Schedule times to watch documentaries and begin looking for places to go and people to follow.

Rather than simply dipping in and out of a subject through a spontaneous Facebook rant, make a plan to learn over the long term. Commit yourself to diving deep, which is why determining a focus area is so important. Will it sustain your interest? Do you feel passionate enough about it? Does it matter? You need to clearly identify a subject that you really want to dig into, versus one about which you simply want to know a little more. That's an important distinction.

There are many times I've come across areas of study, in which others have gone deep, and recognized that I can learn from their deep study without going there myself. I can become more familiar with that idea or position, but I am not interested enough or don't have a good enough reason to dedicate myself to that kind of intense study. Determining where you will dive deep will necessarily force you to get clear on what you will not study.

But once you have narrowed the field, make a plan to go deep. You don't have to commit to being a world-class knowledge shaper—just decide to study this subject until you feel confident in any conversation about it. That might require you to read four books and talk to a local expert. It might require classes. You can determine the depth and the time. But commit. And follow through.

Sixth, I am open to others. When you learn, don't just read or access people who already agree with you, particularly on issues with diverse opinion. Embrace the statement: "I am open to what others have to say." This is hard to do, harder than it sounds, because when we hear or read from people who do not share our core values or suggest strategies with which we disagree, we can have a visceral reaction to them. We can feel like throwing the book away or rejecting it at the outset. But we must all be careful of confirmation bias, of learning only from those who already share our core convictions.

Our ability to help others will be directly related to our ability to understand, and at times even empathize, with people and positions about which we disagree. If we can represent others accurately, and then share why we disagree and suggest other courses of action, then we will have much more influence.

The alternative is too common: define opposing ideas poorly, set up straw figures with which to joust, and then revel in triumph over the foe. And everyone cheers. But those looking on who have more knowledge about the subject or are part of the camp you are dancing over in victory are not convinced and are less open to your influence than ever.

However, if you present an opposing view accurately and justly, representing their concerns and strengths with empathy and grace, and then present your opinions in contrast, you are far more likely to convince and persuade than you would be otherwise.

Even when I hear someone talk on a subject about which I agree—let's say on a point of Christian theology—but do it in a way that maligns and misrepresents dissenters, I am not impressed. Truth is better than that, and we need not be afraid of presenting what we deem as false or opposing positions, accurately. As influencers, we must think and read and learn openly, weighing other positions thoughtfully and truthfully, and rejecting reactionary rhetoric for the sake of greater influence.

How We Communicate What We Know Matters

Before we leave the subject of how our knowledge enhances (and our ignorance detracts) from our influence, we need to talk about how we communicate what we know. How we share our knowledge directly effects how much our knowledge ends up influencing others.

A while back, my son attended a live, online cinematography summit, where world-class filmmakers shared their best work and their most helpful advice. He really enjoyed it. But when I probed more about it, he said, "You know, these guys are really great, but many of them are terrible speakers. I had a hard time following them and ended up skimming through some because they were so poorly done."

Huh. So, let me get this straight: a keen, young filmmaker attends a conference with the best and the brightest in the world, but didn't get as much out of it because *the presenters didn't know how to communicate.* They stumbled around, hadn't arranged their thoughts clearly, hadn't done the work of thinking through how to convey their hard-won experience. And as a result, they were not able to connect with at least one of their target audience.

How you present affects what gets heard, which then directly impacts influence. While you may enjoy tremendous personal growth through all that you have learned, if you cannot communicate it effectively to others, then your personal learning will be of little value in the lives of others. You may be one of the best in your field, able to work in wonderfully creative ways, but if you can't pass it on to others, your scope of influence cannot expand. And this is the burden of this book—that we more effectively and helpfully influence others, be they our own children, our boss, our like-minded peers or our political adversaries.

I talk for a living. Or perhaps I should say, I communicate professionally. I write, I counsel, and I speak, for much of my work. And so, to be effective I must ask if I'm actually communicating what I am intending to communicate. Why? Because I continue to be surprised by how leaders, who will spend so much time honing their knowledge and craft, spend almost zero time considering *how* what they are saying is being heard.

Allow me to use an example from my own work as a pastor who gives weekly public talks. Figuring out what I'm going to say at any particular gathering of the church requires prayer, research, reading, reflection, and writing. I mull and I wrestle and I brood. I write, then edit, then delete, then write some more. At times it comes in a flurry; other times it's like trying to walk through deep, sticky mud. I love it, and there are days when it's a real chore.

But understanding what the Holy Spirit is saying through a particular passage or story of Scripture—knowing *what* God's Word says—is only part of the process. Then I've got to figure out *how* to say it. Or, more accurately, how to help people hear what God's Word says. And that's a step that many preachers, even today, do not work hard enough to do. Which I understand, because after you've used what precious little time you have to wrestle through the meaning of the Scripture, we often have very little energy or time left to really consider how we are going to make this meaning available to others.

But are we being effective in sharing this important, potentially life-transforming truth if we do it in a way that few can even receive? Isn't that just a waste of time? Isn't it an abdication of our responsibility? I think so, though I still talk to preachers who feel that their job is the simply "share" and let the Holy Spirit bridge the gap between what's being said and what's being heard. Well, it's true the Holy Spirit can do that (thankfully), but isn't there some expectation that the communicator would let the Holy Spirit help her or him overcome that gap, seeking effective ways of communicating in the language and worldviews of the hearers of the message? Yes, I think so.

Let's expand this idea, because the same is true for every area we attempt to communicate truth that matters—at home, at work, with friends. We should not be content to just throw out content willy-nilly, no matter how good or true it is, and hope something sticks. Most of it won't. There's way too much information being tossed around. We live in a media-saturated world moving at Mach speed. Look around—more words clearly don't equal more understanding.

We've got to become better communicators, better story-tellers, for the sake of God's glory and people's good. Too many of us think we've done the job of communicating when we've only just begun to put together the truth that must be shared. Let's get practical about delivery, about tone, about messaging, about media, about how exactly we can help others hear and understand the truth which can change their lives, shift their views, and move them toward the life God has for them.

As I have studied and practiced the art of communication, there are seven principles that guide how influencers share their knowledge. These seven principles can be applied equally to a convention speech or a dinnertime conversation. But they are especially relevant for those situations when we are hoping to inspire or initiate change in others.

Seven Principles for Influential Communication

First, people need to feel the need to know. Our initial role in communication is to help create desire. All good communicators assume that they must first convince the person of the importance of what they are saying. But you can't always do that by saying "this is important." You've got to create a desire to know, so that when you share what you have it meets a need others have identified. This requires the communicator to think through what they are saying and how it is meeting a need on the other end, whether they are aware of that need or not.

Often, people aren't aware of the need. When we are sharing some knowledge that we believe will really make a difference in their lives—be it their parenting or their work or their understanding of culture or God or their practice of gardening or cycling—we first create desire. We talk about the things that frustrate us, the nagging doubts we wrestle with, or the obstacles we continue to encounter. We try to get people in touch with their deepest quest for meaning, we try to tease out curiosity, we attempt to build tension that must be relieved, somehow.

And when everyone is ready, when your son or your church or your staff are starting to want to know how to fix this problem, address this dilemma, or resolve this tension, now they are ready to hear what you have to say. Too many communicators share important knowledge that no one thinks they need, even if they really do. Don't assume desire —take responsibility to create it, foster it, tease it out. Assume that the truth you have is important to their lives, even if that's not recognized at first.

Second, people need to believe you're worth hearing. Trust is everything. If people don't think you are credible, if they don't think you understand them, or if they suspect you are selling something you aren't using yourself, then you will not be able to influence them.

And here's the deal: you may well be credible and committed, but if people don't feel that credibility or don't trust that what you are sharing is relevant to them, then they won't be receptive to you. The classic example of this is the boss who seems intent on giving her employees direction, who herself has never done the work they are doing and doesn't actually know how to do it as well as they do. No credibility, no receptivity.

On the other hand, I see people try to share good advice, coming from a wealth of experience and insight, but speaking out of nowhere and never establishing any relational connection. At least at first, people hang back and watch, not sure if they can trust what this person is saying. Usually, if the person really is knowledgeable and experienced, you can see it begin to dawn on people that they can trust this person, and as trust grows, so does receptivity.

The better practice, when you are with people who don't know you, is to take time to establish who you are, tell a little bit of your story, share some of what you've been involved in, not as a way of impressing others but so that they realize that you are someone who is worth listening to. No influence without credibility.

Third, people need to be respected for where they are at. We need to speak with words that people understand. People are not receptive if they feel disrespected, as we will explore more fully in chapter five.

When we communicate, we show lack of respect by either assuming specialty knowledge or by talking down to them as though they are dumb. Both have devastating effects on our influence. Insider language works well only when everyone in the conversation is an insider! When accountants talk to other accountants, doctors to other doctors, farmers to other farmers, all the mutually shared definitions and jargon help the conversation move fast and free.

Try joining one of those conversations as an outsider, and you realize how tough it is to track with the discussion.

But that's not because you are less intelligent—it's simply because you haven't had the same experiences or learned the same vocabulary. Pull someone from that particular group and dump them into a conversation between you and your insider buddies, and they would feel the same way.

Again, that's not inherently bad *unless you are actually trying to influence an outsider.* If you are just shooting the breeze with buddies, go ahead and use all the fancy jargon you want. But if you are trying to help someone change their view on soil amending, public transit, or how early kids should be taught to read, then use language everyone can access, and treat everyone as the intelligent people they are.

When people are respected and included, when a needed definition is helpfully explained but no one is patronized, then the influence of our communication grows.

Fourth, people need to sense resonance with their own worldview and language, even if it's being challenged. We need to use images and language of the people. When we are working in realm of ideas and attempting to create change and inspire movement, we will face push back. There will be ideas and initiatives, actions and agendas, which conflict with the status quo, as well as with other viewpoints and practices.

Knowing that is true means that in order to communicate effectively, we must communicate with words and images that resonate within the worldview and language of the very people we are trying to influence.

An amazing example of this is how John uses the term "logos," which is then translated into "Word." We already quoted this passage above: "In the beginning was the

Word, and the Word was with God, and the Word was God" (John 1:1 NIV). Within the worldview of the people first receiving this story of Jesus, "logos" already had meaning—it spoke of the rational, impersonal mind what was behind everything, the force that made the world coherent. When the average Greek or Roman heard "in the beginning was the logos," there was no disconnect for them. "Logos" fit perfectly into their worldview, with no dissonance whatsoever.

But as they kept listening to John's story unfold, it began to dawn on them that this Logos was different, somehow—that this Logos seemed more personal, and was, in fact, a person. When it all comes home in verse 14, with the Word becoming flesh, we get to the part of the good news story of Jesus that confronts the rational paradigm of the Greek worldview. (Greeks didn't go for the idea that God would get too mixed up in physical creation, let alone that God was personal.)

But notice that by then, there's been a connection, a resonance, a way of speaking their language, then subverted through a clearer definition as expressed in Jesus. Masterful. Like Paul on Mars Hill in Acts 17, we can quote the poets and songwriters of this world to point people to the reality of God. Whatever we are communicating, we need to consider the worldview, the language, the culture of the people we are trying to influence, so that they feel resonance, even as they are being challenged.

The fifth principle of influential communication is that people need to be helped in practical ways. We place other's needs first. Just as we must create desire for the knowledge you are sharing, we need to be helpful in what we say. In other words, we can't set people up by creating desire and then not actually provide anything helpful.

If we are to be truly influential, what we say needs to meet real life, even if that is an idea that helps a person see themselves differently or introduces an affirmation that alters their perspective. The best communicators help people, placing themselves at the service of others. They say and do things that make a difference in people's lives. They orient their communication toward important issues for real people.

Being helpful does not mean being trite, nor is it all about some five-step solution. It means that we are not sharing our knowledge for our own good or to show off what we know; we are sharing what we know or what we are learning for the good of others, meeting real needs and helping them move forward in some important way.

In order to do that, we need to ask ourselves how this truth or knowledge connects to their need, and then suggest questions or actions they can take to pursue further growth. People should feel not only that you were knowledgeable, but that you were helpful to them. Because if you're helpful, you're influential.

Six, people need to be engaged. Always invite responsive action. Everything I've said above could assume monologuing. We aren't. All these principles must be employed in good communication—including, if possible, responsive dialogue in larger forums.

Most of our influence, however, will not be from public platforms. It will be in the one-on-one or smaller group interactions we have at work, school, church, or home. As good communicators, we always want to invite response and provoke questions. We want people to engage what we are discussing, because the more engaged someone is, the more likely they are to be affected by what's being said.

Prioritizing engagement reminds us that all good communication goes both ways, where there is a give and take of ideas, questions, and insights, clarifying what's been said, challenging assumptions, and offering alternative solutions. When we have been given permission to communicate something we know, be that at a coffee shop or a community association, we must push ourselves to ask "How can I most effectively engage these people? How can I help them respond? What action do I hope they will take based upon what I've said?"

In a more formal context such as a public talk, this is easier to think through in advance and structure your speech accordingly; it can be harder to create on-the-spot dialogue from a platform. In more informal conversation, however, it may be more difficult to think through response and engagement beforehand, but it's much, much easier to invite response, listen to the other person's ideas, and have a true, meaningful dialogue. It's called having a conversation. Either way, people need to be engaged so that they can respond. If they've engaged and responded, even in disagreement, then you are becoming a more influential communicator.

And seven, people need to be inspired by a vision for how this truth can change them and change the world. We need to help people imagine the difference truth makes. People need to be inspired by how, if believed or applied or acted upon, the truth or knowledge you are sharing will make a real difference in their lives, as well as in their families, communities, churches, organizations, and businesses.

Vision ties together everything we've done, from creating a desire for knowledge, to sharing truth that resonates and engages and helps. But at the end of it all, we need to raise our sights, to think through how this step or this action or this idea can bring powerful change to our lives.

How does changing the way we think of attachment transform not only our relationship with our kids now, but our relationship with them 20 years down the road? How does grasping our identity as children of a good Father who deeply loves us change negative body image and harmful self-loathing? How can practicing humility lead to incredible changes in workplace culture?

Whatever the point, you want people imagining how the application of this truth would transform their relationships, their self-understanding, their witness of Jesus, the growth of their church, and the good of their communities. The more people imagine the benefit of practical changes, the more likely they are to embrace the steps they need to take today in order to get there. And that, in the end, is what good influence is all about.

In order to influence others, we must be in rigorous pursuit of the truth, committed to personal growth and continual learning. Getting a bigger head isn't the point. Though we do experience personal transformation through the learning we do, we want to pass on this transformation by becoming effective communicators of the knowledge and truth we are receiving. When we do, we become more influential than ever.

Reflection Questions

- Can you think of a time when a person's knowledge helped or hindered their influence?
- Of the six personal statements for cultivating knowledge, which one do you find most inspiring personally? How will adopting personal statements such as these help you?
- When you reflected on the questions designed to narrow our focus, was there an area of learning that surfaced? How will you do pursue that?
- When you consider your communication (personal or public), where are you the strongest? Where is your growth edge?
- What is your greatest danger when growing in knowledge?

3

HUMILITY

Humility is not thinking less of yourself;
it is thinking of yourself less.
- C.S. Lewis

Pride goes before destruction,
a haughty spirit before a fall.
- Proverbs 16:18 NIV

We've all felt it. We're bopping around a party, and then find ourselves cornered by the smartest person in the room, and they'd like us to know it. Once I knew a young man keen to share his greatness with everyone, in every conversation. And while I felt some empathy for this fellow, I could also feel his repulsing effect on me and see clearly his fallout with others—his pride drove people away. Not only did people not want to associate with him, they began to actively resist him, even when the things he said were technically correct. His arrogance destroyed his influence.

Few things are more repellent than pride. Something within us pushes away from arrogance. Coming off a chapter on knowledge and the importance of learning, it is appropriate that we would now look at the centrality of humility. Because knowing more doesn't always have a positive effect. More knowledge can inflate our sense of self-importance and significance.

The Apostle Paul warned that "knowledge puffs up while love builds up. Those who think they know something do not yet know as they ought to know" (1 Corinthians 8:1-2 NIV). In order to stave off pride, we've got to get intentional about humility.

In the end, it doesn't matter what you know if you are unable to use that knowledge in helpful ways. But if you are prideful about that knowledge, arrogant about your ideals, then your ability to help others is severely compromised. People don't like to be influenced by people who think they are better, even in areas where they might be. Pride diminishes influence.

Why is that? I think it's because most of us know how small we are and how little we know. Average people know a few things moderately well and feel like they are floundering in most other areas in life. I know that's how I feel. Talk to me about two or three subject areas, and I can get pretty animated because I feel some measure of confidence. But expand beyond that, and I am floundering out of my depth. And, usually, I know it. (I've also had the horror of discovering my ignorance sometime later.)

Enter someone who feels that they really are better and smarter than me, and I react. Why? Because pride and arrogance make me feel small, insecure, and stupid. And, like clockwork, defensive and resistant. (Surely I am not the only one?) Even if we could learn something, our insecurity and defensiveness shuts us down. Feeling waves of pride makes us less open to their knowledge and influence—not only do we feel protective and vulnerable, but our own pride kicks in. Some of us want to fight, to show off, to react. We start resisting because we don't want to feed another's pride even more. In fact, we want to cut them down to size, however possible. Influence, gone.

Seth Godin, in his little book *Poke the Box,* tells the story of Hungarian doctor Ignaz Semmelweis, the pioneer of antiseptics in surgery. Semmelweis, horrified by the high mortality rate among postnatal women, embarked on a quest to discover why.

Before the time germs were understood, medical students would move directly from infected patient to newly-birthed mother, thus spreading disease and causing widespread death. Through the process of elimination and serendipitous discovery, Semmelweis became convinced that washing hands with a chlorinated lime solution between patients could help, and excessive mortality rates dropped to virtually nothing within two months! Stunning.

Imagine, just for a moment, how significant this discovery was, how potentially life-changing to the whole practice of medicine. But, as Seth relates, Semmelweis was unable to create widespread change, partially due to his unwillingness to explain his science to anyone (his own lack of understanding of why his method was working may have contributed to that lack of explanation).

But more than that, Semmelweis was a prideful jerk, berating his colleagues and belittling his opponents. His life-saving practices were eventually adopted after he died, based upon the confirmation of germ theory by Louis Pasteur and successful implementation of his work by practicing surgeons. But don't miss the point: Semmelweis was onto something absolutely true and vitally important, but he failed to influence others in part because of his pride and his lack of respect (see chapter 5). And while we can understand his frustration and anger and exasperation at the resistance of others, we can't deny that he was at least partially to blame for his inability to create change. If he had approached others with a little more humility, if he had been willing to think through how he could best influence without alienating, how many more people would have been saved? Pride kills influence. And in this case, pride even killed people.

Humility, on the other hand, is attractive. Have you ever been around someone who surprised you? That person who was so unassuming, the one who kept asking you the questions, making you feel smarter, encouraging you to talk. And then finding out this person is fabulously accomplished but doesn't seem enamoured by their own abilities or gifts? If you have, then you know what I am talking about. When that happens, your willingness to learn from this person spikes. Their humility built a platform for their influence, even though they very likely did not intend it that way. That's the thing about humble people: they aren't using their humility to influence others. They are humble, and therefore, they influence.

I can hear what some of you are saying right now—it feels like a Catch-22. "How does a person focus on humility and not fall into the trap of feeling good about their progress?" Yes, there can be pitfalls. If we want to grow in humility, how would we even measure that growth? And if we did, wouldn't we fall prey to the very thing we are trying to avoid? But knowing that danger can keep us working on a more accurate view of ourselves, developing a humbler stance. We will look at some practices for growing in humility toward the end of this chapter.

Humble people honor others. They do not focus on what they know, but on how they can serve others. When you are humble, others are surprised with what you know, surprised with what you have to offer, because you were not caught up with showing them how smart you are. And when that happens, people end up asking you for more, wanting you to share.

In the presence of a humble person with a depth of knowledge, people will often hold themselves back and ask you to speak. And if they don't (and we've all been around folks who are unaware and just press on to share their own knowledge) then no problem—they weren't open to your influence anyway. And that's okay.

Humility is also a key to influence because a humble attitude invites further conversation. When a person is humble, they model an attitude that others will pick up on, inviting humility from others, modelling a stance of learning that others will adopt. As such, humility can powerfully shape a corporate and organizational structure. And in a culture of humility, people don't feel like less; they feel like more.

It is somewhat paradoxical that in a culture of humility, no one feels humiliation. Rather, people feel more honoured, more encouraged, more built up, whereas in a culture of competition and one-upmanship, people feel lost and less-than. In humble cultures, people feel more inclined to learn, to cooperate, to stay connected with one another and with you.

In our last chapter, we explored the importance of our knowledge to our influence. But the danger of knowledge is that as we grow more knowledgeable, we could begin to look down on others who know less. Or, perhaps, we simply see ourselves as the real gift to the organization, and our self-perception erodes our influence.

The fact is, becoming truly knowledgeable—even attaining expertise—doesn't require arrogance, and we must war against that in our own hearts and minds. An intentional and rigorous posture of learning and growth is not about just knowing more, amassing facts or skills for the sake of accumulation.

Growing in knowledge, though deeply personal, is not about us—it is about shedding light on current problems and issues. In other words, knowledge is about influence, but if we adopt ways of knowing and sharing knowledge that prevent us from having greater influence, the very purpose of our knowing in the first place has been lost.

Knowledge should be gained for the sake of something beyond ourselves, something we want to see changed or a value that we want to see instilled. Knowledge, then, is about serving others, helping others, advancing a cause and a solution.

In the verse we quoted above, knowledge which puffs up is contrasted with love which builds up (1 Corinthians 8:1-2). But if knowledge is placed in the service of love, so that its goals align with the building up orientation of love, then knowledge can serve without naturally puffing us up. In order to do that, we need to be part of something bigger than ourselves, compelled by a vision greater than our own agenda or subject to our own pride.

Another area of danger to our humility is subtler—we must be watchful in how we model our convictions. Integrity is essential to influence—we've already covered that. We must live out what we believe with intention and consistency and transparency.

But the related danger to that integrity is that we become pretentious models. Ironically, if we are not aware of this danger, even our attempts to help others live with more integrity can undercut our influence. When we begin to see ourselves as examples of integrity, even as paradigms of faithfulness, we are in danger of pride. When we begin to view ourselves as a little too right, we can fall into the trap of self-righteousness.

This can be seen in so many ways, and from areas as varied as effective parenting, conscious consumerism, creation care, healthy eating, or any other right or good practice we can name. If we begin to offer ourselves and what we do as the answer to everyone's question, the solution to everyone's problem, we will become repellent instead of compelling.

Imagine a couple who does a great job parenting, raising great kids, with truly a lot to share about effective and sensitive parenting. Honestly, we could all learn from them —in every way, they model a way of parenting that is good and helpful. The problem spawns when they *begin to see themselves as such great models* and, instead of waiting for others to ask them to share their parenting insights, they began to offer it in ways that made other parents feel worse about themselves. And this can be so subtle, and so pretentious. A little comment here, an "oh, here's how we do it" there, and people began to resist. I ask you, did their pretentious modeling help or hinder their influence?

To change the example, we've all had that friend who is ultra-disciplined in their exercise and eating habits, who always seems to be on top of all the things you struggle to even remember. How helpful was it when they, seemingly innocent to how it makes everyone around them feel, hold themselves up at the ideal to follow? "Oh, just do what I do." How does that make you feel? Warmly invited to grow, or villainous in your own pride and insecurity? Yeah, I thought so.

The truth is, without humility, without grace enough to wait until people ask, without the self-awareness that pride can seep into all of us, our modeling can become pretentious and off putting, killing any influence we could have had.

Growing in Humility

So how do we practice humility? Or more to the point, how do we grow our humility, without becoming self-conscious about it and feeling good about it? As the old joke goes, "I won a humble pin, but they took it away when I wore it." How can we do this?

First, we need a bigger mission. Serving something larger than us decentres us. We are not the point, and it is only through a conscious and intentional pursuit of purposes larger than ourselves that we will take our eyes off ourselves and fix them on something bigger, something that demands we be better, that we grow larger, that we serve more effectively, that we lay ourselves, along with our gifts and talents and resources, out on the table for something greater than us. When I know I am not the point, then I'm less likely to begin thinking that everything is all about me.

Second, we need a better reference point. When it comes to knowledge or influence or growth or failure or struggle, I must stop living in reference to myself. I live in correlation to something larger, or more accurately, Someone larger. I live as a human image of the God who created me, dethroning myself, yes, but also equalizing others in relation to me. If I can do that, then I won't live in comparison to others around me, either good or bad, smarter or dumber, more informed or ignorant. Those categories no longer apply, as I am no longer measuring myself by how another is imaging God, but how I am imaging God. My criterion for life is the One I was designed to reflect. I look to my Creator and serve in reference to him. That has a powerful way of growing our humility.

Third, and very practically, we need broader learning experiences. We can grow our humility by purposefully choosing to be a novice at something. By choosing to be a perpetual learner, there is always some place where we are the uniformed, we are the ones who are clueless, the one who will make the dumb mistake, the one who causes snickers for the foolish assumption.

What's the advantage here? The novice learner knows how clueless they are and know that they do not even know how much they do not know. And as a result, they are humbled before others who know more and must, awkwardly and openly, submit to the leadership of others. This might be the teen teaching you tech, the farmer helping you plant or the new immigrant teaching you her home language.

Incorporating this position of novice is not just for new things within your areas of strengths—for example, an athlete learning a new sport or a professor learning a new philosophy. No, to be a true novice, step outside your natural strengths. This is the one good with words now learning small engines, or a person who easily learns physical skills now picking up foreign language.

Whatever it is, humility grows as you choose learning that pushes you into areas where you feel incompetent and foolish, where you need the help of a child, or worse yet, the help from someone that, if the situations were reversed, you would tend to think of as your intellectual inferior. These are city slickers working a ranch, professors trying a skate park, or rednecks enjoying the symphony. We only grow outside our comfort zones and humility naturally results from stepping out.

The truth is that we can always learn something from someone. And the people around us, even the people we had subtly looked down upon, know many things that we have never learned.

When you come to realize and believe that everyone can teach you something, then you can adopt the stance of the novice learner, the curious questioner, anywhere and everywhere you go. That takes humility. And, in a way that will surprise you, your stance of humble learning from others will honor them, raise them up and nurture your relationship with them in such a way that, you will find your influence growing, even in areas not related to what you are currently learning, and you didn't even know it.

And, fourth, we need brutal self-examination. We must be willing to ask ourselves hard questions or be open to questions asked of us. I've become more and more convinced that cultivating self-awareness through intentional reading, journaling, reflection, spiritual direction, counseling, and conversations is a critical success factor for our relational growth and influence.

There are just way too many business owners, civic leaders, pastors and parents and politicians, who are unaware of their character gaps, oblivious to their off-putting vibes and awkward assertions. And it's killing their influence.

What's more (and it is more), it's keeping them from really becoming who God created and called them to be. Their lack of self-examination and awareness is debilitating their marriages, their health, and their spirituality. Enough! If we want to lead, if we want to grow, if we want to help others, then let's get serious about growing inside, about addressing who we are internally, where the real mess resides. And when it comes to the most hidden darkness of all—pride—we are going to need every ounce of brutal self-examination we can muster, and then some.

When I was forced to look at my pride honestly, it changed my life. I say "forced" because I didn't choose to look—someone else had to hit me hard so I could finally smell what was stinking down inside.

Passionate about my Christian faith, I had become insufferably self-righteous. I was raised in a Christian tradition that, though loving and gentle in so many ways, was also very clear on the "rules" of religion, particularly when it came to the big four taboos—drinking, smoking, dancing, and gambling. There's some fascinating history on why those four areas of ill-repute got so much focus, as well as the church's role in fighting those evils, but I was unaware of all that and grew up judging people for those four and more.

Now, I don't want to caricaturize anyone, not even myself. I experienced so much grace and encouragement and support from this community, and I owe my very life to them. But we were a conflicted community—as a teenager I was torn between showing grace to "sinners" and pronouncing God's judgment on them.

And, more than I care to admit, we'd only show grace if people responded with repentance when receiving our judgment. The result was a growing pride in my own heart. And the more I got things "right" in my own life, the worse my pride got, because it's easy to feel better about yourself when you are comparing yourself to others who are constantly screwing up. And, of course, as someone who felt he was getting it right, I felt it my duty to help others "get it right."

If I had been asked, I would have said I was humble, of course. It's just that others were wrong and needed my help. Yes, you can imagine how much people loved that help! And then one day, a day I'll never forget, a friend who was actively resisting my "help" finally snapped and started yelling at me.

We were standing in his kitchen, arguing about something that that he needed to change (in my humble opinion, of course!). And then, into my face with such force I can still feel sparks, he bellowed, "You are so self-righteous!" I was stunned. It was like he'd hit me in the head with a hammer. Everything within me recoiled at this crazy accusation. I wanted to deny the charge, to defend my humility.

And yet, within moments of his outburst, I knew he was right. I had become a self-righteous little rat. I had become the very picture of a biblical Pharisee. And that challenge on that day was the rock in the rut, lurching me out of one trajectory and setting me on another.

I began exposing myself to more rigorous self-examination, exploring ways I had become prideful, arrogant, and totally insufferable. Ways I had begun to see others as stupid or sinful or wrong or immature, and then to think of myself in more generous and aggrandizing ways. Oh, I had filtered all of these harsh judgments through a very Christian lens; it was all about holiness and purity and serving God. But inside, deep down, I was feeding a growing pride, expanding a darkness that would threaten my life if ignored. I am so thankful for the day my friend lost it on me.

How did I begin to deal with this horrifying realization that I was prideful and self-righteous? Not by attacking it head on. You see, through my teenage years, I had adopted Solomon's prayer from 1 Kings 3, where God appears to the newly installed King Solomon in a dream, inviting him to ask for anything he wanted.

Now, Solomon could have treated God like a genie, asking for gold or longevity or power. Instead, Solomon asked for wisdom—the wisdom needed to rule the people of God. His request was rooted in humility, acknowledging his own lack and inexperience, but the main request was for wisdom. God honored Solomon, knowing he could have asked for so many selfish things.

Inspired by this story, I prayed for wisdom, asking regularly for God to grant me "a wise and discerning heart" like Solomon's. Was that a bad prayer? Was it inappropriate? No, I don't think so. In fact, I'd like to say that God responded to my prayer, granting me wisdom and insight as I pursued a growing relationship with him and as I devoted myself to mission and to Scripture study.

But something happened as my faith grew, something unexpected and something God didn't want. I also grew in pride. I began to feel that I did know more, that I was being blessed by God, that I was more mature than the average kid my age. This concurrent growth of pride alongside the growth of wisdom is not that strange, when you think of it. In fact, if you map out the life of Solomon, you can see how these grew simultaneously in his life, too.

But at some point, something breaks, and pride wins the day. And the wisdom long nurtured and God-given begins to wilt and dissolve, even leading a person into folly and destruction, as it did in Solomon's own life. His life stands as a biblical parody of wisdom, where the wisest and most knowledgeable man in all of history falls prey to the stupidest and most basic of spiritual traps. Wisdom grows us, but pride can destroy everything wisdom built, if we aren't careful.

So, by God's grace on that day in 1991, horrified by who I had become, my heart prayer shifted from "God, give me your wisdom" to "God, make me a person of grace." Instead of desiring more knowledge, I wanted more grace. I wanted not to be known as a person who knew lots but as a person who loved lots. I wanted to have a heart shaped by the love Jesus had for others. I wanted people to feel God's grace through me.

Now, God's grace in me is still a work in progress. I run across judgmental Tom more often than I'd like, so hear me clearly when I tell you of a time when I did realize that God was making progress in my life.

Fast forward a few years and picture an argument between the best of friends. I can't remember the actual situation, but the essence of the conflict was my unwillingness to write someone off who probably deserved it. I was arguing for giving them another chance, trying to give more grace. And, out of the blue, my friend says to me in exasperation, "Tom, it's so frustrating how you refuse to see the bad in people. You always want to see the good in people instead of admitting how awful they are!"

Now, obviously that wasn't an entirely true statement—I was still seeing the bad in people, quite able to focus on the negative, and would readily acknowledge ways people were less than stellar. But on that day, perhaps 3-4 years after my prayer had shifted from my desire for wisdom to my need for grace, I realized, with surprise, that God had been answering my prayer. That though I was nowhere near getting it right all the time, I was, more often than before, seeing people with a more gracious heart.

Why do I share this? Am I at risk of feeling proud here? If I weren't so challenged by how judgmental I still am, perhaps I would be. No, I'm simply illustrating my point: it wasn't by attacking pride head on that I was able to experience change. While many things can be addressed head on, I'm not sure pride can be. If we focus on it, pride can be reinforced even as we fight it.

Rather, it was as I pursued something different—in this case, God's grace in my life—that God was able to root out the pride and produce the grace he longed to grow in me. And through that second argument with my good friend, God suddenly tapped me on the shoulder and said, "See, I am at work in you. You are growing in grace. Now keep on growing!" Still am, still need to.

Following the Humble King

The truth is, true humility will grow in us only insofar as we get close to someone who is both far greater and humbler. Jesus, in whom all knowledge and wisdom and strength is perfectly present, lived in complete humility and kindness toward others. His very life was a demonstration of God's grace to others. In the words of the beautiful hymn of Philippians 2, Jesus, who was God, didn't cling to his position at our expense. "Instead, he gave up his divine privileges; he took the humble position of a slave and was born as a human being. When he appeared in human form, he humbled himself in obedience to God and died a criminal's death on a cross" (Philippians 2:7-8 NLT).

Mediating and reflecting on Jesus' greatness and humility, and then worshiping him as the humble king, creates space in us for his humble, transforming work in us. Jesus is now the risen, exalted king, the one who is now elevated to highest honor, as the following verses in Philippians 2 reveal. And yet, by his Holy Spirit, the humble king Jesus now resides in us, too, leading us and directing us and humbling us, in all grace, so that we, too, can be humble like him. And that humility matters, in both personal and practical ways.

Proverbs 16:18 famously states that "Pride goes before destruction, a haughty spirit before a fall." And we can think of all the ways that pride can destroy us on a grand scale: the loss of a business, the fall of a marriage, even the destruction of a life. But I'd like to apply this verse to our conversation about influence, that the more pride we have, the haughtier our spirits become, the more our influence will be destroyed in the lives of others. The more we esteem ourselves, the less we will create meaningful change in our organizations, our churches, our business and our families. A haughty spirit destroys influence, but humility grows it.

If we are to be influential, then we must become more self-aware of our own dangerous pride, more vigilant about the state of our self-righteous hearts. We must let Jesus grow his humility in us. Because whereas humility is winsome, pride is repellent. And if we want to influence others toward a greater vision, toward a grander purpose, then we must humble ourselves.

Reflection Questions

- Where have you seen pride hurt influence?
- How can we guard against pretentious modeling?
- How do you practice regular self-examination so that pride can be identified, confessed, and subverted?
- What bigger mission helps you combat pride?
- Who has humbly influenced you?

SECTION TWO

FOUR INDISPENSABLE INTERPERSONAL QUALITIES

Our Care Determines Our Influence

Our ability to influence others towards growth and wholeness will be helped or hindered by how we treat them. Without the four interpersonal qualities of empathy, respect, grace, and love, we will never help others experience all that God has for them.

4

EMPATHY

Be pitiful, for everyone is fighting a hard battle.
- Rev. John Watson

Seek first to understand, then to be understood.
- Stephen R. Covey

We have explored three key ways we must grow ourselves in order to grow in our influence. The more intentional we are in self-leadership, the more influential we are as leaders. The more we grow personally, the better we can help others grow personally. Our integrity, knowledge, and humility form the foundation upon which our influence is built.

But where do we go from there? In this next section, I want to explore four interpersonal qualities which will either enhance or destroy our influence, and they contain some of the most important chapters of this book. Seeing these four realities in play, both within myself as well as in relationships around me, motivated me to write this book.

We move from a focus on self-leadership to our care for others. The way we care for others has the power to make, or to break, our influence. We begin with empathy.

What is empathy? Empathy takes us behind the scenes of someone's life, where we can see from their vantage point and feel from their perspective. Empathy involves understanding why a person believes what they believe, acts as they act, fears what they fear, and loves what they love.

Empathy is not sympathy. Sympathy is about feeling bad or good about what another person thinks or has experienced, whereas empathy moves us in close, so that we can more experientially "get" what a person is all about.

Empathy gives people the benefit of the doubt rather than jumping to suspicion and mistrust. When we are empathetic, we make daily decisions to move toward people rather than away from them. We resist our natural tendency to keep enemies at bay. Instead, we get in close and try to understand, to listen, and to see.

What happens when we fail to empathize? Without empathy, impact is muffled. People don't feel heard or understood by us. And when they don't feel heard or understood, then whatever decision we make or action we suggested doesn't feel applicable to them. You don't understand my situation, they think, because if you did, you would not suggest what you did. Your failure to empathize has hampered your ability to influence.

Without empathy you will not achieve the kind of buy-in needed to move anything positive forward, be that with your teenager, your church leader, or your co-worker. People feel a disconnect and will resist any efforts to create change. But if we will work hard to see things from another's perspective, to feel their heart, to look through their eyes, then we are much more likely to move others to see through ours.

Without empathy, we are not able to love people as we should. We don't know them, we don't know their story, and we end up acting out of our own interests instead of theirs. Furthermore, our failure to empathize makes us more likely to disrespect someone, or to fail to show them grace. Our conclusions about them are faulty, and we make snap judgments about their character based upon actions and words lifted from their storied context. Without empathy, we risk alienation and misunderstanding. Empathy is essential to influence.

Four Reasons We Fail to Empathize with Others

So why are we often so unempathetic? There are at least four reasons.

Perhaps one of the greatest reasons we fail to empathize is that we do not want to affirm what the other person is saying or doing. When a man spouts ugly rhetoric about a certain political position—and especially if the position being slammed is your position—it is difficult to remain calm and seek to understand the man's perspective.

Instead, we want to push back, hard. We feel that by asking them why they believe or think as they do, they might take it as support. At a Christmas party, a man mumbled political opinions that I found reprehensible, involving violence toward a woman as a solution. I was angry. My face flushed, and I lashed out.

In that moment, all I wanted to do was fight, to shut him down and call him out. I was very unempathetic. I didn't care why he felt what he did—I only wanted to fight. Empathy felt like a soft, weak stance.

However, I am not much of a fighter, and I wolfed down more pie in an effort to collect myself. I choked out a searching question between bites. I strained to listen, biting back retorts, and I heard the story motivating the anger.

Turns out, this man had lost his job because of political decisions made, and he was deeply worried about providing for his family. Already several months out of work with no clear prospects, his fears, piled on top of personal regrets for his lack of vocational training, had led him to a place of helplessness tinged with violent rhetoric.

Now, I strongly denounced his statements. I disagreed with his interpretation of what was happening. But (and this is crucial), by listening to him I was able to better understand why he was responding as he was. Rather than fighting at the level of his fear and worry, I was able to speak into the hurt and the fear and pray for him, believing that his rhetoric, though still reprehensible, was an ugly symptom of greater pain and fear.

We can think that empathy means we always agree, but the truth is greater than that: we are able to empathize with someone without agreeing with them. We can ask probing and insightful questions, aimed at understanding and uncovering the person's hurt and fear and convictions. And when we do that with love and grace, we are then able to speak more effectively into their life than had we just rose to a fight.

The second reason we fail to empathize is that we are more eager to be affirmed than to understand. Parents can be guilty of this when they want their kids to do what they are told while at the same time failing to listen and understand their objections.

One of our sons often pushes back when he feels he is being misunderstood. He wants us to understand him and why he is struggling with something we've been telling him. He's not an especially rebellious kid, but he desperately wants not to be misinterpreted and misheard. Only by slowing down enough to listen and care about the way he sees things are we able to empathize and he feels heard. And I can tell you for a fact: he's much more open to our direction when he feels he's been heard and knows we've cared enough to listen.

The third reason we fail to empathize with others is that we are moving too fast. We simply don't take the time required to ask, listen, and understand. Practicing empathy is slow work. In order to hear someone's pain, to listen to someone's story, to get alongside someone struggling or resistant, we must slow ourselves down. By re-prioritizing our schedules, listening begins to happen throughout our lives.

When we are too busy to listen at that moment (sometimes, the kids really do need to be picked up and that flight really is leaving), then we must be willing to make a note and come back to them, to text or call and set up a time for further conversation. Let's not fail to empathize just because we didn't make the time. That's the equivalent of saying, "You don't matter to me. I don't care enough to make understanding you a priority."

And here's the crazy thing: we can be so busy doing

good stuff! Pulled along by serving and prioritizing other people, it can be hard to slow down when we most need to.

One of the stories of Jesus that challenges me so much is the story of the bleeding woman in Mark 5. Jesus has been pulled into an emergency situation—a 12-year-old girl is dying, and Jairus, the desperate father, has sought out Jesus and begged him to come and heal her.

Can you think of anything more urgent? Jesus responds quickly, and they begin working their way through a clamouring crowd of Jesus' admirers. It's hard slogging, as the streets are narrow and the people are packing in as close as they can to Jesus.

But on this day, anonymously hidden among this crowd, a woman comes who is just as desperate as this pleading father, a woman who has been hemorrhaging blood for the entire lifespan of this little girl.

Imagine that, bleeding for 12 years. Not only is that a debilitating medical problem, her bleeding made her a social pariah. According to Jewish religious law, her condition rendered her ceremonially unclean, excluding her from much social and religious life. Her presence that day in the crowd was itself a violation of the law, because everyone who jostled against her in that excited crowd was, by definition, made unclean upon contact, even though they didn't know it.

But she ups the ante even further. Not only is she making people unclean, she then reaches out and intentionally touches Jesus' robe, believing that by doing so, she would be made clean again.

Remember: as the story goes, this woman has tried everything to get better. She had endured horrible remedies at the hands of experimental physicians, with no positive effect. She was getting worse and was broke from trying to get better. Unclean, unhealed, and at the very end of her resources, she courageously acted in faith by pushing through that crowd and touching Jesus.

Well, if you know the story, you know what happens next. Jesus, who is on this very important mission to heal a dying child, stops everything.

"Who touched me?" he asks.

What a joke. Are you kidding Jesus? Everyone is touching you! We are in a squeeze here and have been pushing people out of the way to get you through the crowd. But no, Jesus was serious.

"Who touched me?" he asked, because he had felt healing power leave him, and yet could not figure out who had been healed.

"Who touched me?" At that moment, this poor woman knew the game was up. But she also knew, wonderfully, unbelievably, that she had been healed. Coming forward, falling at the feet of Jesus, she tells him her whole story.

As she stammered out her tale, I can just imagine the crowd recoiling from her, suddenly creating ample space around this unclean-yet-claiming-now-to-be-cleansed woman. And Jesus listened.

How long did her tale take? The story moves fast—Mark, the gospel writer, is known for the way he clips through stories. But this woman, having bled for 12 years, trying this, attempting that, going there, hiding here—she had quite a story to tell. And Mark relays that she told Jesus the whole truth.

Jesus listened with such empathy, and when he had heard her full story, he didn't condemn her for having broken the law; he commended her for having faith in him. And his deep empathy leads him to say, as her tale is complete, "Daughter, your faith has healed you. Go in peace and be freed from your suffering" (Mark 5:34 NIV).

This story is so rich and textured, but I want to hone in on only one aspect here. While Jesus was on his way somewhere else, the need to care for someone arose. He could have just gone on, and the woman would have been physically healed. But it was only as he stopped, letting her come out of hiding, tell her whole story, and be publicly commended and restored, that she would be *socially* healed —restored to her larger community as well. Jesus not only healed her through an unintentional touch, he healed her through intentional empathetic listening.

Remember what else was happening? Mark tells it using a popular "sandwich" technique, relaying this story within the still larger framework of the dying, little girl. Or shall I say, the now-dead little girl. For as Jesus was listening to this woman's whole tale, however long it took, the 12-year-old girl did actually die.

Imagine how her father felt as he watched Jesus stop, insist on knowing who had touched him, then taking the time of which his daughter had precious little left to listen to this woman. Can you feel his stress? His mounting anxiety? Perhaps frustration, even anger, at this woman for her interruption, or possibly at Jesus for his seeming disregard for what's really important, for what he had already agreed to do? Because it is "while Jesus was still speaking" that people arrived from Jairus' house to tell him it was too late. His daughter had died.

While Jesus took the time to listen to one person's story, another one had ended. Oh, I can't quite imagine what Jairus must have felt at that moment. But Jesus knew.

Despite his willingness to take the time with this woman, he hadn't forgotten about Jairus or his daughter.

In fact, this delay, which must have looked like so much devastation when Jairus stood in the middle of that shoving crowd, would result in something even greater than he could imagine: Jesus raised that little girl from the dead. Could this be what Jesus knew all along, that his empathy for this woman, which transformed her life, would also have a transformative effect of Jairus, too? That would be just like Jesus, wouldn't it?

The fourth reason we fail to empathize is that we feel defensive about our own position. Perhaps we worked hard to provide something great for our colleagues, or we thought through an initiative for our serving team at church, only to have someone react negatively to our suggestions. We can feel hurt or misunderstood, putting us on guard. When we feel defensive, it is hard to listen empathetically. We feel vulnerable. We try to explain ourselves. It takes grace and courage to remain open to others when you are feeling attacked or disregarded.

So, what do we do in those cases? We remember that even good change is hard for some, and how we react in the moment will help or hinder that change coming into effect. And so, we acknowledge within ourselves that we are feeling slighted, or misunderstood, or defensive.

And then we apply the sage advice to "seek first to understand, and then to be understood." We ask questions, non-defensively. We probe the reason for the pushback. We invite dialogue, and we remain open.

Now let me be clear: choosing empathy does not mean we say nothing, absorb every criticism, and never challenge reactions. But in those moments, instead of going on the offensive, can we lean in to empathy and seek understanding first? There's a reason why people are responding the way they are, and the more you can understand that, the better you will be able to lead needed change. If we will guard our reactions and invite connection, then we will be surprised at how much people are able to accept and change.

Becoming More Empathetic by Listening Well

So how do we become more empathetic? How can we grow in our ability to see through other's eyes? By becoming better at listening to people's stories. For it is only through stories that we come to see and feel and know, from their perspective, what is important, what creates fear, and what guides their hearts, minds and priorities.

One of the holy privileges of my pastoral work is hearing people's stories. Many are deeply private, and I am humbled by how hearing stories changes my perception and grows my love. The more I hear what people have endured and the struggles which have made them who they are, the more I understand the choices they have made, even the damaging and harmful decisions. An old friend of mine used to say, "Don't judge me for my limp today without asking me about the truck that hit me a year ago." But so often, we don't know that story about the truck, and so we lack empathy for the limp.

And so, if we are to grow in empathy, we must tune in to stories—open to hearing, truly and deeply, what has brought someone to where they are today. When we do, we will be blown away by the grace evident in their story, by the weight of their story, and by the way God is at work. We will judge less and love more. We will see why she has struggled to find someone to love her unconditionally and why she continues to make harmful relationship decisions. We will come closer to understanding why he always hides his emotions in conversation, coming across as cold and uncaring when down inside he desperately wants to show love and express passion.

When, instead of judging a person at face value, we assume a greater backstory, we are then able to lean past some of the very things that push others away. From a person's body odor to the ways they look perfect, we can move past the barriers and listen to the reality of brokenness and the movement of God's grace.

The truth is, this has helped me become more empathetic, even when I do not yet know the story behind the person's actions or attitudes. The more I hear people's stories, the more I assume that everyone I know has a story, even if I haven't had the opportunity to hear it yet. And that makes me more inclined toward an empathetic and gracious stance in advance of their story.

We must do this in our personal relationships, intentionally cultivating our own skill as listeners. For some of us, this comes very naturally. I watch in awe as a friend of mine asks question after perceptive question in social gatherings, making those around her feel great about themselves and wonderfully drawing out their personal stories. She is a master in the art of conversation, sprung from a deeply empathetic heart. By the end of the evening, the people around her feel incredible—they feel heard, loved, and special. And that is so significant.

But can I also make a larger point? By the end of the

evening, having been heard and loved and encouraged, everyone would walk across Lego blocks for this empathetic, kind woman. Her influence expanded because of her empathy.

So how do we cultivate our skill as listeners? As I reflected on my friend's amazing hospitality, I discerned four essential practices which guide her empathetic listening, and these four have helped me become a more empathetic listener, too. Let me share them with you.

Four Essential Practices for Empathetic Listening

First, be present. Even though there are many causes for distraction, my friend keeps present to others. Even when she is hosting a party, managing the food and drinks and hospitality, she is oriented toward those who are with her. She will invite them to help her in what she is doing, all the while attentive to them.

The take home for me? I must intentionally focus on the person who is right in front of me. While that might seem obvious, I can't count how many times I've been meeting with someone and caught myself thinking about my next appointment, all the while pretending to listen to the person in front of me.

Over a decade ago, I felt Jesus challenge me on this, and I decided that, in order to love the person I am meeting with, they need to be the most important person in my life for that particular moment. For some of us, that means leaving our phones alone, refusing to fiddle with them during conversation (in fact, why not put it away?). For others, try sitting in a way that will minimize distractions, like not facing the door or window. Sit forward, remain intent, choose presence.

Do what you need to do to fix your attention on the person you are with, whether that's your kid, your spouse, your friend, or your workmate. The person in front of us is loved by God, created in his image, important, valuable, and worth hearing. I want to treat them that way and by remaining present in my mind and heart, I can do just that. Be here now.

Second, be inquisitive. My friend asks great questions, flowing from her genuine desire to know the other person. What I've picked up from her is that, in order to listen well, I must curate good questions. Not only does that keep me engaged and present to the conversation, but open-ended, curious questions invite people to talk more about themselves and what they love.

It's such a wonderful gift to others, giving them permission to talk freely and enthusiastically about themselves. Many are never asked to do that. Now, I realize that for some of us, like my friend I've been learning from, asking inquisitive questions on the spot comes quite naturally.

What about those of us who are not as good on our feet, who can't think of what to ask in the moment? You can prepare a little in advance. Does that seem weird? I have another friend, also gifted in the art of hospitality, who frequently invites diverse groups over for shared meals. She knows these folks are strangers, and so she takes a few minutes before they arrive to think about a couple leading questions for each person, just to prompt the conversation should the meal suddenly get quiet and awkward. And if that happens, she peeks at a little note she's jotted down and placed under her placemat where no one can see (I'm not kidding), and asks a question to one person, perhaps about their line of work or something they've been involved in, and away goes the conversation again.

People are so rarely engaged with interest by others, and many are longing to be heard. When you hang with people who are intentionally inquisitive, you realize at the end of the evening that you've talked a lot, you've been heard, and you feel like a million bucks. I want people to feel like that when they talk to me. By being inquisitive, we become better listeners.

And third, be humble. Apply what we discussed in chapter three on humility. Specifically, don't be afraid to say in the middle of the conversation, "I don't understand what you are talking about. Could you explain that to me?" You can't listen well if you don't understand what's going on. Sometimes we don't ask clarification questions because we think things might become clearer as the conversation continues. Fair enough. But if things aren't clearing up, call a timeout and go back.

Other times, though, we fail to ask for clarification because we don't want to admit we haven't seen that movie, didn't know that bit of news, or can't quite get what they are saying. Just own up to it. Embrace the novice role. Pride will not only stunt your ability to listen, but it'll hinder your ability to learn.

Confused about something? Try re-stating what's being said to see if you're getting it right. If you aren't, your friend or colleague or son or daughter will love explaining it, especially if you are already asking open-ended, curious questions about something they love. You'll find that people who employ obscure medical terms or arcane theological jargon or geek talk or hunting lingo are willing and passionate teachers. Speak up and ask.

Finally, be thankful. You know what I love? Hearing my friend thank people for the way they have shared with her. She's so real and compelling and genuine, and the people (who have already fallen in love with her) almost blush under her gratitude. Do you think I'm exaggerating? You should see her in action.

How has her thankfulness affected me? When I've heard someone share their story, be in in my office, at a coffee shop, or in the middle of a bustling party, I always try to say thank you.

Thank you for sharing your story with me.

Thank you for your courage and honesty.

Thank you for telling me about that situation.

Thank you for explaining that to me.

Thank you for the honor of hearing you.

If I can, I tell them specifically what I appreciate, how I've been challenged, or what I've learned. When we do that, we show how much we value them and how our listening to them has been an expression of our love.

In the end, I want to listen well so that people are loved well. And for these four listening practices, I am so thankful to my friend's example as I attempt to practice them in each conversation.

Moving beyond the realm of personal relationships, we can also cultivate empathy through reading other's stories (memoirs, biographies) or seeing movies and documentaries based upon people's lives and experiences. These are wonderful ways of becoming more attuned to others, even people so far away from us, inhabiting such different space and time.

The more we can see life through another's eyes, the more practiced at empathy we will become. A recent podcast I've been listening to focuses on this kind of empathetic listening. On *Intersections with Rose Zacharias Meeder*, Rose invites people to share their story, and it's a wonderful experience of listening. She intentionally draws them out, and her love for her guests (many of whom are her personal friends) is evident. And then, in the context of their story, she invites them to reflect on faith.

Rose is a committed follower of Jesus, but her guests come from a variety of religious and spiritual backgrounds. Hearing them share their faith journey, in the context of their story, is powerful to hear. And not only does Rose model intense empathy, we become more empathetic as we hear the stories of people we've never met.

But it's not only other's stories we need to hear—we must also become better listeners to our own story. Does that surprise you? Many of us have never made the space to consider our own journey. And by reflecting upon—by *listening* to our own stories—and then writing them down, our empathy grows in a few ways.

First, we become more aware of our own influences, our own reasons for thinking and doing what we think and do. We are also able to identify patterns of grace and sin, choices made by us or for us that have affected our own lives. We see how events have changed our direction, how people have hurt or helped us, ways our family of origin has shaped us, and how God was always in the mix.

By doing this kind of listening work, we grow in our ability to empathize with ourselves, so that we are not just blindly acting but are now more in touch with our own heart and emotions, identifying our own influences. And by becoming more aware of our biases and actions and influences, we will become more gracious toward ourselves and more open to others. Understanding why I do what I do will go a long way toward understanding why others do what they do.

So, what's your story? Take a month and begin detailing your critical moments and influential relationships. Use a mind map or plot them on a timeline, with your locations, jobs, significant friendships, defining events, emotional/mental/physical health, spiritual journey, etc. See your own story open up before you, noting the special as well as the horrible moments. Step back and notice patterns. Become fascinated and inquisitive about your own story.

And then write it up. As you do, share it with a trusted friend who will support you. Ideally, invite someone else, or better yet, a small group of friends, to join you in this personal narrative project. Let go of idealistic literary expectations—you are not trying to write a best-selling memoir (though some of you might, and if you do, I want to read it!). You are writing for you.

But then share your stories with each other; read them and reflect upon them. Ask more questions of each other and affirm each other and the grace you see evidence in their story. It's a powerful, life-changing experience. And in the end, you may find that your ability to empathize with others just might be connected to your ability to hear your own story.

There is always more going on in someone's life than meets the eye. God is at work, weaving in and out of the bumps and folds of our lives. And each story is holy as a result, for each story points to the grace of God. Are we willing to get close and listen? Are we game to see through another's eyes, so we can truly empathize with them? Our influence is directly proportional to our empathy. Because when we touch on the deeper stories, we will not only more fully understand others and ourselves, we will be more understood by others.

Empathy breeds influence. Very practically, the more empathy we have, the better leadership decisions we can make, be that everyday family decisions or massive organizational ones.

In the now-iconic movie *National Lampoon's Christmas Vacation,* Clark's boss, played by Brian Doyle Murray, cancels the Christmas bonuses to save money. His decision, made without reference to the real-life effects it would have, in his words, on the "little people," lead to a string of hilarious events involving a kidnapping by cousin Eddie and a full take-down by the local SWAT.

When confronted with the ugly truth and realizing how his decision to cut the bonuses had been made without understanding and empathy, Mr. Shirley reversed his decision with grace. How many times have we done the same, within our work or at home? The failure to empathize not only diminishes our influence but sets us up to make poor choices without full context. But the more empathy we have, the more people will be open to our help and influence.

Reflection Questions

- Of the four reasons given for our failure to empathize with others, which one do you most identify with? What other reasons might you add to the list?

- How have you grown as an empathetic listener over the years, and where are you being invited to deepen that now?
- How has understanding your own story helped you become more empathetic toward others?
- Consider the statement "I want to listen well so that people are loved well." How does that challenge or encourage you? Who in your life needs to be heard so they can be loved?

5

RESPECT

So God created human beings in his own image.
- Genesis 1:26a NLT

You have never talked to a mere mortal.
- C.S. Lewis

Whatever your political perspective, we have endured a grinding *tour de force* of disrespect in recent years, thrown up on the big screen of our society. As a Canadian, I have witnessed this disrespect grow in the national, provincial, and local spheres. As a Canadian with American family and a deep love and respect for the American people, I have watched the last few years of political drama unfold with concern.

We have seen a level of disrespect in dialogue escalate, in ways few can remember. And the toxicity, often hidden from polite society, has spilled over into conversations among neighbours and friends and church members, both online and in person.

And the results are in: disrespect kills influence. The more I observe, the more I am convinced that we cannot influence people we disrespect. But it's more than just that, because not only are we unable to influence the people we disrespect, but our disrespect for particular people fans out and diminishes influence in other people's lives, the ones who might sympathize with those whom we disrespect or are just put off by our lack of decorum.

This is critical. I'm convinced that if we don't address this lack of respect in our own lives, we will see our good influence diminish. We will not be able to guide our children, we will not be able to help friends see with new perspective, and we will not be able to encourage changes where they are needed the most. If we are willing to be disrespectful, then we are choosing to minimize our influence in a world that desperately needs good influence.

The Foundation of Respect: People Are Images of God

To restore respect for others, we return to the very basics: who we are as human beings. The foundation of our respect is the fact of our humanity: we have been created in the very image of God and we are worthy of respect because of that status.

In Genesis 1:26, the creator God makes a stunning decision: after making a good world filled with wonderful creatures, God decides to create beings in his own image, in his very likeness, beings who are part of the created order and yet destined to provide caring oversight of creation, beings who reflect in their very nature and relationality the being and nature of their creator God.

Being images of God roots our attitudes and actions toward others. How we treat each other, even how we privately think of each other, stems back to who we are as people who image God, people stamped with God's who-ness and reflective of God's nature.

As the story of Scripture goes, humanity's fall into mistrust, rebellion, and violence did not eliminate the divine image (Genesis 9). Though it has corrupted our ability to live as images of the true God, we continue to reflect God's divine image even in our sin and struggles, as well as in our relationships, our art, our invention, and our way of doing life. Like shattered glass, we reflect God still, though poorly.

Does the fact of our sin or our corruption as images of God mean we are less valuable? God didn't think so. In the most famous Bible verse of all, a verse many of us could recite, we are reminded that God loved the world so much that he sent his one and only Son, Jesus Christ, to make restoration from our brokenness and forgiveness of our sin possible (John 3:16). It is while we were still sinners that Christ died for us (Romans 5:8).

If the Father, the Son, and the Holy Spirit deemed us valuable enough to die for, sinful as we are, then surely we can accord each other respect as loved images of God, regardless of how different we are or how much we disagree. God's love sets the standard for our respect.

We must remember the purpose of our personal influence: it is to help people reflect more truly the image of God they truly are. If our influence is to be any good, it must serve others, oriented toward people receiving healing and forgiveness and grace, for the sake of their restoration as fully integrated, vibrantly-reflectional human images of God. In this chapter, I argue that unless we respect all humans as images of God, we will not be able to bring the kind of good influence essential to any human flourishing and growth.

One of the reasons people struggle to show respect for others is that, like empathy, they fear showing support. But showing respect for others as human images of God does not mean we agree with that person's ideas or that we support their actions. We may hate what they are doing; we may even say that a person has even become someone terrible, falling far beneath their God-imaging potential.

But our opinion of them can't simply be based on our likes or dislikes, our preferences, priorities, or even morality. Our opinion of others must be rooted in the larger reality: even this person, even one so deformed and wretched, even one so frustrating and toxic, was created by God to be an image of his nature in the world.

Whatever they are now, they were created to be more, more than they have become, and if I am to have any chance of helping them toward the restoration of their original nature, then I must see them for who they are *and* who they can become, which is greater than any sin or rebellion or ugliness. Again, God's loving action sets the standard for my respect.

In reality, though, there are very few people we can't respect in some way, even if there are things about them with which we profoundly disagree. And in those moments, we must also look for attitudes and actions that we can affirm, strengths we can nurture, ways we can encourage.

But all of these are rooted in the basic wonder that, as C.S. Lewis famously said in his essay *The Weight of Glory*, "You have never talked to a mere mortal." Each one of us have been created in God's divine image and must be accorded the dignity and respect that goes along with that, even when we must, at times, work overtime to do it.

Two Ways Our Disrespect Disables Our Influence

First, our disrespect disables our influence on others with whom we disagree. When we show disrespect to people with whom we are at odds, we reduce our ability to influence them to exactly nil. We might disrespect them because we don't like them and they irritate us, or because we profoundly disagree with their political persuasions, their theological views, their parenting style, their stance on sexual orientation, or the way they carry themselves. Whatever the reason, disrespect disables influence.

When we fail to show basic respect for people with whom we part ways ideologically, there are a number of things that happen. To begin with, our nasty mockery or derisive rants makes us look petty and immature, so unlike the character of Christ. I cringe when friends who should know better post nasty and mocking comments on social media—it makes them look bad, cheap, less than I know them to be.

But then something else happens. Emboldened by the disrespect, others join in the shredding and make it even worse. Comment threads get mobbish. And if you are a follower of Jesus, then these words are now bringing disrepute to Jesus, because (big surprise) how we treat others directly impacts how others view Jesus.

Failing to show respect also short-circuits good, healthy conflict, because the issues that need to be discussed become overshadowed by the ugliness of the conversation. You and I have both seen it. People who feel disrespected dig in defensively, hardening into their positions. Even if you were able to give compelling argument for a reconsideration of their views or actions, your disrespect killed that possibility. No one has ever been won over by being beaten down.

The reality is, when we show disrespect toward others, we end up harming our relationships with them. People feel unheard (there's lack of empathy again), and therefore very much less inclined to agree with your finely developed and rigorously expressed articulations. You won't influence a hard-working farm kid from Alberta if you think he's a redneck idiot, nor will you influence a software-developing hipster from New York if you think she's a clueless liberal. Lack of respect leads directly to lack of influence.

And so, all theological reasons aside, a compelling, practical reason to show respect for others is that you can't bring change without it. If we are to offer help or provide leadership for people who are not all like us, then we must foster respect and uphold the dignity of each one, keeping relationships real and vibrant. This does not mean we don't talk about areas of disagreement or dissonance, but it does mean we do that within a framework of fundamental respect.

To ensure this kind of respect in the home, workplace, or church is to establish ahead of time *how* we will do conflict together. We can set up agreed-upon rules for our inevitable conflicts. In our church community, we developed a "behavioural covenant" outlining clearly defined and mutually accepted ways of grappling with each other when things get hard.

The best time to develop these rules are not in the middle of the mud-slinging match, but when enjoying a picnic on a summer's day. (Though if you find yourself stuck in the mud without some common ground rules, calling a timeout to establish some will be helpful.)

Over a series of months, meetings, and prayer, we established seven key practices which would define our conversations and conflicts in our community. Rooted in Scripture, these seven practices are regularly read, visually displayed, and periodically preached. They include such statements as "We commit to intentionally believe the best in each other; to listen wholeheartedly and patiently; to communicate with clarity, compassion, and truth; and to use words that honour each other and build each other up."

And so, when we are struggling with a particular issue or person or dircction and we are tempted to turn to disrespect and derision, we hold up our agreed-upon terms and encourage ways of conflict that remain healthy and God-honouring. The sad truth is, if more churches had decided ahead of time how they would handle conflict, there would not be as many tragic church splits or harmful stories to tell. Similar covenants have been developed for workplaces and homes, to good effect.

Second, our disrespect also disables influence with others beyond our awareness. Disrespect not only disables our influence in the lives of the people we despise; it also disables our influence in the lives of others around us, the people silently watching us deride or dismiss, mock or make fun of our opponents.

I find this second rung of lost influence deeply compelling, because I've witnessed this phenomenon in profound ways within the church and family space. An older Christian who would otherwise demonstrate care and respect for people in their relationships, turns and speaks about "those" people (a politician, a group, folks who live a certain way or hold a certain ideology) in very ugly ways. They don't articulate their care for the humans involved or the causes they support; they don't distinguish between the "sin and the sinner" as it were. They just pontificate about the evil without remembering the good.

Let's get more specific. When a teenager wrestling with sexual identity overhears a Christian man make derisive and hurtful comments about LGBTQ people, how likely will it be that this teenager seeks safe conversation with this person? When a millennial wondering what God has to say about creation care then overhears a barrage of vitriol about some politician's stupidity regarding a carbon tax, is it likely that this millennial will seek further guidance from this Christian?

This is so important. If you mock people who hold an opposing position, your ability to influence others around you who are grappling with the very issues involved is harmed. If you caricature another's position without any empathy for why they believe what they do, you cripple your influence.

Young people around you are silently watching, even within your own household—do they see respect, or rage? Your fringe friends on Facebook or new-to-faith folks you just met at church may be quietly withdrawing from your influence. Why? Because your position is wrong? Maybe, maybe not. It might be because your lack of respect for others has overshadowed the truth of your position. How we interact, even with those who are not in the room, will affect our ability to influence others who are in the room.

Everything we've explored so far comes into play here. Respect is founded upon empathy (chapter 4), for without empathy, it will be difficult to respect others. But respect is also firmly rooted in who we are as people, transparent and authentic about our own journey (integrity), growing in knowledge and understanding of not only our own ideas, but also other positions (knowledge), and doing so in a humble way (humility). You could almost say that respect is a natural byproduct of these first four things.

Over the last decades, we have seen the rise of polarized political and social debate. Lines have hardened, and disrespect from opposing sides has become vogue. Within each sphere of relationship, from the kitchen table to the coffee shop, from the boardrooms and schoolrooms to the streets and farms and hills, we are witnessing the demise of common respect.

Mock someone's hair and you get cheers of support. Make filthy comments about a person's look or stance or position and, in some venues, you might even see a rise in popularity (notice I said popularity, not influence).

What we are seeing is the triumph of ugly rhetoric over thoughtful argument, where certain people use any means necessary to demean an opponent, in an effort to win at all costs. But the cost is too great—the cost to our humanity, the cost to our society, and the cost to our Christian witness.

In the old Latin, we have made the argument *ad hominem*

(against the person) rather than about truth, beauty, or goodness itself. And while those who are attacking the person will often say that they are doing so because the person's character is so closely tied to the issues, I fail to see in this an argument for vicious disrespect or infantile mockery.

Now don't get me wrong. I believe there is a place for satirical comedy in society; through comedy we are able to poke and provoke in ways we are normally unable to do. But there is a line, and I think when we move away from satirical comedy and into outright ugliness we have moved from provocatively helpful to potentially harmful.

This is increasingly evident on social media, that platform for all things poisonous and polarizing (as well as funny cat pictures and helpful tutorials). Our diminishing respect for one another is front and centre on these platforms, particularly if you've ever fallen into the cesspool of the comment section on any politically or socially charged post.

Our online behaviour is hurting us as a society and harming our witness as Christians. If we are to have any positive influence toward a better world, then we need to seriously check ourselves and our online behaviour.

It is so easy to mock others for their convictions. It's much more difficult to move them toward new ones. And if we want to move others towards anything, then mocking them won't help. Nor will it help us become the kind of people worth being influenced by. Name calling, mockery, and abusive language should be considered unacceptable by any follower of Jesus, the same Jesus who said that "a good person produces good things from the treasury of a good heart, and an evil person produces evil things from the treasury of an evil heart. What you say flows from what is in your heart" (Luke 6:45 NLT).

If that's true, then we need to have our hearts checked. We need to take seriously Paul's inspired directive: "Do not let any unwholesome talk come out of your mouths" (Ephesians 4:29a NIV), or better yet, "Don't use foul or abusive language. Let everything you say be good and helpful, so that your words will be an encouragement to those who hear them" (Ephesians 4:29 NLT).

This seems to have come into particular focus in our behaviour on social media, where the perceived anonymity and distance has allowed for, or perhaps perpetuated, disrespectful speech. The ranting and abuse we witness online is having a direct impact upon our daily witness as Christians, and it is harming our ability to influence others.

Perhaps we should rephrase Ephesians 4:29 to read, "Let no unwholesome typing come out from your fingertips," for the more we demean others who think differently, the less likely we are to understand their position or affect any influence. And on a public platform such as Facebook, many, many others are watching what we have to say and how we are saying it. And what they see is having an effect.

Why is it so hard to talk about important issues on social media? Here are at least 5 reasons why.

Five Reasons Good Discussion Falters on Social Media

First, the lack of relationship. Whether it's about environmental policy, church strategies, or the latest food allergies, debates often rage between people who have no relationship with each other. Maybe the conversation started between friends, but then the threads were quickly hijacked by folks who do not know or love or understand one another. And with the absence of relationship comes the absence of nuance, caring, and empathy. And the demise of fruitful conversation.

Second, the larger context is missing. More than once I've witnessed a showdown between two people who, if they had known each other's story, would have been much more careful and thoughtful in their responses. But this comment or that bullet didn't allow for that, and eruptions followed. When I am in relationship with someone, I understand more of what's behind the screen, and how I talk and respond and even challenge them changes as a result.

And third, there is no accountability. This is a big one. Perhaps nothing stands out more than how digital platforms create the illusion of anonymity, even if our names are posted right beside our comments! And with that illusion comes a lack of accountability. With our fingertips, we say things we will never be forced to backup (we can just log off). There is no real way of holding to account someone's ugly tirade or hateful comments, barring a little bit of shaming or blocking a certain user.

Fourth, little trust exists. Another reason meaningful dialogue seems difficult online is the lack of trust people have for each other. Given what we've said so far, it's understandable. No relationship + no context + no accountability = very little trust. And, yet, for a true exchange of ideas to occur, especially important and conflicting ideas, we have to extend some benefit of the doubt to the other person. We can't think the other person is just an idiot. As others have taught us, such as Patrick Lencioni with his *Five Dysfunctions of a Team*, trust is foundational to good conflict over important ideas. But I see very little trust on the social platforms (and often for good reason).

And the fifth reason? Limited time. This one may surprise you, but I think the fifth reason conversations are difficult online is that we are often engaging in an ongoing thread of debate or discussion while moving at disorienting speed. We are commenting on this political idea while holding a bag of nails at the hardware store, then sniping in on someone else's parenting comment while our own kid is demanding lunch.

We just haven't slowed down enough to engage, and we end up reading too fast, commenting too quickly, failing to understand the issues, unable to follow through and then wondering why everyone's so upset. Some of these conversations just can't be engaged within the time it takes to descend from the 4th floor of our office building.

I've been reminded of this many times in my work as a pastor. Not only do I have to be careful in what I like, share, and say online, but I have seen how what others like, share, and say online affects real life relationships. People post having no idea how a person they've been befriending from church is disturbed by their online rants and sentiments, mainly because they haven't yet heard the depth or pain of their story.

But now that they have posted such disrespect, will they ever have the opportunity to hear that story? Or has their online behaviour shut down the possibility of more vulnerability and transparency in their relationship with this other person? I know for a fact it has.

Furthermore, what kind of influence is actually happening? I, for one, do not see anything helpful coming from the spewing disregard or the mocking disdain that has come to characterize much online interactions.

People, especially Christians, who think they are standing up for the truth and getting people to see the light but are resorting to the kinds of speech that they would rarely, if ever, use to a person's face or in regular conversation, need to realize they are doing much more harm than good. Rather than initiating thoughtful dialogue, they are creating further division and polarization—and lack of respect is often at the root.

And lest I sound like a pandering softie, having respect doesn't mean we don't speak up. We must be willing to lean in and have difficult conversations about the real issues facing us. Being respectful is not code for the avoidance of all conflict—but it is a call to engage that conflict with wisdom and grace, in light of human dignity and relationship. What we say is not the only consideration; when we speak and how we speak is paramount.

So how do we determine when to speak and how to speak? Many of us have never thought through how to engage in good conflict, and I'd like to suggest seven filter questions that can help us do so. Running through these seven filter questions, either in advance or in debrief, may help us as we consider when and what we should be saying, both online and in person. Remember what James said? "Anyone who is never at fault in what they say is perfect..." (James 3:2b NLT) Perfect. Well, we are far from perfect, but perhaps we could get better? I think we can.

A Seven-Point Checklist for Respectful Conflict

First, have I listened well? Before we dive into sharing our ideas or opposition, we do need to start back in empathy. Have I even heard what's being said? I so often just dive in and start slinging.

But how many times have we reacted strongly to something we've misunderstood, when, by listening a little further, we might have discovered that we hadn't heard the whole story? Or more likely, by listening first we'd be able to better respond to the person we are actually talking to, and not some caricature we've dreamt up or some other person who said a similar yet different thing. It can be hard to slow down and listen when the heat gets cranked up. In order to respect another person, we need to start by listening well.

Second, is it true? My words need to line up with the truth. Yes, this can be very tricky—everyone speaks from a personal vantage point and we need to ask ourselves if we are representing the truth, or just part of it. Do I have all the facts? Have I understood what's going on? And what does the Scripture say? Followers of Jesus appeal to the Holy Scripture as our final authority, but that does not mean that simply quoting a Bible verse makes what I am saying true. As one of my seminary profs used to say, "Just because it's in the Bible doesn't make it biblical."

Southern slave owners in 1830 used the Bible to prove their rights to own, beat, and even kill other human beings —were they being biblical because they could quote the Bible? Men have used the Holy Bible to support domestic abuse, a use of Scripture that is sick and destructive, not holy or true.

Less dramatically, we can be guilty of simply stringing

together a few verses, which, out of context and mashed together, seem to make a very biblical argument, but in their original setting would not support our theory. I must ask "Are my thoughts, ideas, and perspectives true?" I must be more concerned with the truth than my own opinion, and my words (and questions) must demonstrate that. Humility is necessary.

Third filter question: is this conflict worth it? Let's be honest: there are times when the issue at hand is not worth the fight, either because the issue is not worth causing trouble for, or the timing is just wrong. We need to be wise in our evaluation, discerning the value of the conflict.

Sometimes the fight is worth it—the dignity of other people is at stake, there is potential for lasting harm, or it's time to lean into something we've been avoiding. But there will also be times when we hold that larger concern (say, helping this person find Jesus) as far more valuable and choose to let go of a smaller issue (say, what they think about a particular social issue).

Fourth, will I be understood? Similar to evaluating the worth of a conflict, there are times we know in advance that our words will not be understood. Perhaps there's just too much baggage around an issue, or the emotions are already too high, or we know that this person or group is unable, at this time, to be open to what you would say. We may choose not to create further conflict because we know it will not be helpful or understood. This takes wisdom and discernment, but there will be times when we know our words won't be heard. Respect them and stay silent. Hopefully another day will come.

Fifth, how will my words or actions harm relation-

ships in the future? This is a big one, and one that I see lacking in many online engagements. "How will this rant affect my relationships in the future?" Or perhaps the better question might be, "Will this enhance my relationship?"

When I see Christians post extremely negative opinions about Muslims, as a way of warning others about the dangers of Islam, I always wonder how many Muslim friends they actually have, and what that kind of post will do to their relationships with them? The sad truth is, most posting these kinds of things don't have any Muslim friends, so they are not aware of how much it would damage it would do.

There will be many times we choose the wisdom of silence for the sake of future relationships. We choose "perfection" (James 3:2) today for the opportunity to influence tomorrow.

Sixth, do I have a reasonable chance of success? When we have built trust with someone, listening well and showing respect, we have a much greater chance of influencing them. But if we think that our relationship is not ready yet, if we are not sure if we have much chance of influencing them yet, better to keep building, asking, hinting, listening.

The goal is influence, not rhetoric. We aren't arguing for truth so we feel good about ourselves; we are advancing truth in order to help people embrace truth.

And seventh, is this the right platform? Use wisdom in where and how you engage in difficult conversations. We can see the fruitlessness of much online dialogue. Though there are healthy exceptions, usually within an online community with strong shared values, I'm beginning to question whether we are even able to have these kinds of difficult conversations through online platforms. Perhaps we are, and we need you to lead us forward in that.

But there is still wisdom in asking, "is this the right place or platform in which to engage this particular topic?" Because it well may not be. The truth is, I will be bolder and more caring and helpful over coffee than I will be online, primarily due to the relationality of a face-to-face interaction and the ability to nuance, show love and respect, protect privacy, and listen well, compared to online interactions.

In truth, there are always going to be people and positions that provoke disrespect in us. Certain people feel repulsive; particular beliefs are repellent. All of that is true. But the higher call of influence is that we keep our heads and hearts about us. And if we are to influence others toward truth, beauty, and goodness, then we must not stoop to half-truths, ugly speech, and awful behaviour.

Respect starts right in the heart. Our reason for respecting others cannot simply be a desire to influence them, as though we only watch what we say from our mouths or type online, but we pay no attention to the vile and disgusting ways we view or speak privately about someone else. The challenge of Jesus still stands: what is coming out of our mouths defiles us, because it comes from our hearts.

So, what's in your heart? Are there certain people who just make you want to puke? To mock or deride? To reach for the basest of disgusting rhetoric, so that you feel good when you've had a chance to vomit your vitriol? Then that, my friend, is a *you* problem, a heart condition, and the only remedy is through confession and repentance, letting the

Holy Spirit shovel out the manure and replace your mind and heart with fresh, clean hay.

Empathy will help you grow in understanding. Humility will support this move. But only when you are willing to admit your lack of respect due to any human image of God will you see change come in your heart.

One important strategy for overcoming this kind of disrespect and disdain is through prayer for the person or persons with whom you have a problem (more on this when we explore the importance of love in chapter 7).

Perhaps you have struggled to respect a certain political leader: begin to pray for their hearts and minds, not in a demeaning way, but praying the Scripture over them, praying that "they would know how wide and high and deep and long is the love of Christ," that they would have wisdom and grace and discover the life only Jesus offers. You can't disdain for long someone you pray God's desires over.

Are you having a tough time showing respect for the mother of a child in your son's class, the mother who seems oblivious to the ways her child is hurting yours? That is very difficult. Choose to pray for her, for her child, for her relationships, for her heart and mind. Pray that she could come to understand who she is as one who is loved by the Father and pray that she would have wisdom as a parent. Your heart will shift from disrespect to an attitude appropriate to one who is created in God's image. And you will be so much more ready for the conversation that needs to happen when it does.

Be willing to ask yourself some hard questions: Why do I reach for disdain and mockery whenever I see this or that person? In what ways have I written people off, and how can I increase my love for them? Of course, there will be positions and beliefs that we fundamentally reject. Can't we be disrespectful to the position people hold, we may wonder? In one sense, of course we can. There are vile ideas and despicable positions worthy of our utmost repudiation.

However, in my experience, we have difficulty distinguishing between our disrespect for a position from our respect for the persons holding that position, so caution is needed. It is better to work hard to fully understand a position (the self-discipline of knowledge) and why it's being held (the practice of empathy) so that we are able to engage the person who holds that position with insightful and truth-revealing questions, pointing them toward why you believe what you believe and how that meshes with your fundamental views on being human, caring for the earth, loving God, and living with integrity.

Be compelling in your own vision, articulating your own position so well, and with such deep understanding of theirs, that you become more influential. Many times, it's far better to side-step a direct confrontation over an issue with a winsome and compelling presentation of your own position.

If we really want to influence others, we must rise above the common, mucky bog, refusing to sling the mud, even if we are getting splattered by others. We must lead by example, which can be very difficult. We will find ourselves leaning into empathy and getting run over. We will ask thoughtful questions and receive stunning push back for even asking them. Our attempts to hold respectful dialogue will be hijacked by those who refuse to do so.

In all this, we will be tempted to hit below the belt. And the truth is, if we've really done our homework, we might be able to take out an opponent with unsavory tactics that would be celebrated by our colleagues.

But at the end of the day, will we have increased our influence in ways that are helpful, or will we have just furthered the demise of healthy conversation and good influence? And will we have led others whom we influence to do the same when they are in conflict situations?

To grow in influence, we must grow in respect. Everyone is worth it, because every human image of God is worthy of respect.

Reflection Questions

- When have you seen disrespect harm influence?
- How is our respect of other people connected to our understanding of who they truly are as images of God?
- Disrespecting someone directly diminishes our ability to influence them. But what about people who witness disrespect? How do you see influence diminishing in unseen or secondary ways?
- Social media conversations are often disrespectful. Of the five reasons given for that, which one is most difficult for you? How will you engage conflict online?
- Review the checklist for respectful conflict. How does these questions help you as you consider engaging a sensitive or polarizing subject?
- Pulling everything together so far, how do the three areas of personal growth (integrity, knowledge, and humility), combined with the practice of empathy, enable more respect-filled engagement?

6

GRACE

Accept one another, then, just as Christ accepted you, in order to bring praise to God.
- Romans 15:7 NIV

Without grace, good influence falters. We may dictate to others, we can cajole and demand, manipulate and pressure, but we cannot influence in a way consistent with the heart of Jesus nor the growth of others.

I don't know about you, but I resist people who speak down to me or don't seem to care about my story. People without real grace are people without true influence. Oh, they might be able to push others around, but to provide true influence, where people are being built up and empowered into a fuller life? That's not possible without grace.

What is grace? The theological definition is favor without merit. In other words, getting good things without working for them. We are thankful for God's grace to us.

We don't have to earn God's love in Christ—it's given to us freely.

For the purposes of this chapter, however, I'd like to envision the practice of grace in our relationships as *continuing to give of ourselves to others even when they give us back ample reasons to quit on them.* Practically speaking, grace means that we keep showing up, keep forgiving, keep believing, even when it's hard.

This kind of keeping-on grace is never easy. When we have been walking alongside someone for a while, encouraging them toward healthy, God-honoring decisions which will result in new and better things for them, and then they fail, we feel very upset. We are disappointed and discouraged and a bit hurt.

Some of that hurt and disappointment is because we know how these poor, unhealthy decisions will hurt them in the long run. And, if we are honest, some of the hurt and disappointment we feel is about us—we feel jilted, ignored, and foolish, as though we've wasted our time or that we have been the ones rejected.

In Ephesians 4:32, Paul urges followers of Jesus to "Be kind and compassionate to one another, forgiving each other, just as in Christ God forgave you" (NIV). The ultimate reference point for our forgiveness of others is God's forgiveness of us.

But have you ever noticed the verse, which comes right before this one? Prior the command to show compassion and forgiveness there is first the command to "Get rid of all bitterness, rage and anger, brawling and slander, along with every form of malice" (NIV). When someone else has failed, and they are most in need of forgiveness and compassion, we can feel very angry and bitter about it. We can feel tempted to speak ill of them to others, and even to do things that would hurt them. And we do that because we feel hurt and betrayed.

When I work with someone for years, and then they do something that cuts all of that work to pieces, destroying their marriage, their body, their relationships, and their witness, I feel angry. I can resent them. I want to write them off and forget about them—what a waste!

But here's the question: Will I ever be part of restoring them, helping them pick up the pieces and get back on track if I give into that ugliness? I mean, I understand the natural inclination to write people off—I certainly feel it.

Practically speaking, though, will it help? No, not at all. In fact, as we all know, that rage and anger and bitterness will not only not help them, it will hurt us. There's just no way to hold that stuff without getting hurt ourselves. So, Paul says, "get rid of it." Toss it. Junk it. Haul it to the dump. And not just some of it—all of it: bitterness, rage, anger, brawling, slander, along with every form of malice.

And then the next step? Be kind and compassionate. Notice that Paul doesn't say "wait until you feel some kindness and compassion in you and then act on it." If that were the case, we'd all be waiting a long time. Nor does Paul say to make sure they grovel for a bit before you extend forgiveness. No, we are to *be kind and compassionate.* We are to take action. Make compassion real and concrete.

Wow, that's hard. When we want to fight, but instead we hold out a hand to help. When we want to rage, but choose instead to speak words of life. When we want to savor a little more bitterness, but instead we choose to let it go and forgive. When we want them to feel the pain they've caused us, but we choose to listen again. And how do we do that? By first recalling how we were treated by the Father, so that we are able to forgive *just as in Christ God forgave you.*

And that, my friends, is the key. We cannot embody God's grace for others until we've grasped God's grace for us. Let's go there, because without remembering our own need and experience of grace, we really can't talk about offering grace for others.

Grace and Sin, Sin and Grace

To understand about grace, we must talk about sin. We've got to dig into the ugly truth about our own nasty selves. As followers of Jesus, sin and grace are things that we say we believe, but when it comes to extending grace to others who have failed, we can easily forget the grace we have received.

Sin, as it's widely defined, means missing the mark. If you can imagine setting up a target 50 yards away, and then trying to hit that target with an arrow or bullet but missing it every time, you begin to get the meaning of "missing the mark." Missing the mark defines so much of our lives. Try as we might, we seem unable to live up not only to the good God desires for us, but even to the good we desire for ourselves.

When I was a kid, my eyes were bad. But the problem was, I didn't know it. In fact, if asked, I'd proudly tell everyone I had 20/20 vision, eagle eyes. Well, 12-year-olds in Alberta, Canada can start packing guns and hunting game. And you did not need to pass an eye exam to do so. Are you beginning to see a problem with this? I could only vaguely see what I was shooting at, especially as the distances grew.

One fall morning, I was taken out by a friend of a friend to hunt. He was an experienced hunter and was happy to show a young buck how to get one. There were a few of us out that early dawn, and after walking for only a quarter mile, we stumbled across a herd of deer, emerging from a mist-covered field. And sure enough, among the herd stood a beautiful buck.

This was my chance! My guide set me all up to bag my first deer. But... I had trouble seeing exactly where it was. My guide could see clearly, but I couldn't. My guide said to take the shot, but again, I couldn't quite see it. Yes, I could see there were deer there, and I was narrowing in on the buck, but it was all a bit fuzzy.

I could sense my guide's frustration growing as the moments passed. I was starting to feel hot with shame. I couldn't see. Suddenly the buck sensed our presence. Head came up, froze for a moment, and then he started to move.

"Take the shot! Take the shot!" my guide whispered urgently. He could not comprehend what was taking me so long. "It's right there! Shoot, shoot!"

I couldn't see it. I couldn't see anything. Finally, there it was... BOOM!

Are you nervous yet? Don't worry, this isn't a tragic story. It's not even a bloody one. The fact is, I "sinned" by yards, missing that buck by an Alberta mile. Ashamed, frustrated, and not happy at all, we continued on with what became a totally unsuccessful day hunting. Good thing I was too blind to see all the sideways looks I got.

"Sin" means missing the mark because of exactly that: try as we might, we can't hit the target. When I was twelve, I couldn't help but sin on that misty morning. Why? Not because I didn't want to hit the deer. (Oh, I wanted to!) Not because the gun didn't work. (I assure you, it worked.)

The problem was that I couldn't see. I had a problem I didn't know I had, and it prevented me from doing what I actually wanted to do. The target was right there, in plain sight. I was positioned to bag it, simple as that. But I was unable to see and therefore condemned to miss, all the while wondering what the problem was.

And here's the point: Our choice to reject God blinds us, and because we are blind, we can't hit the right target anymore. But we don't even know we're blinded.

God says, "Love your neighbour," and we miss that target.

God says, "Honor me," and we miss that target, too.

God says, "Do to others what you would have done to you," and... whoops, clean miss.

God says, "Love your enemy." Do I even need to mention how much we miss that one? (Actually, not sure we even try to hit that one.)

Here's the crazy thing: We can't even keep the rules we ourselves say we should follow! We can't even do the good we know we should do, let alone live the life God calls us to live!

And our sinning, our missing, our decision to reject God's life plan brought death right into the good world God created to live! Thankfully that's not the whole story. The good news is this: The God who created us for life wasn't willing to let us just keep on dying. That's the grace of God in action. And the Bible says that we are all in need of God's grace, because each one of us rejected God's loving leadership in our lives.

God created humans to image him in the world, but our

mistrust of his goodness and rejection of his favour resulted in sinful brokenness for all spheres of life. Sin penetrated deep into the four relationships we've already discussed. Our relationship with God was broken, our relationship with each other fractured, our relationship with the planet strained, and even our relationship with our own selves became fraught with confusion.

Brokenness now characterizes our world, internally and externally, and as sinful people living on a groaning planet, we perpetuate brokenness in everything we do. Hear me right: our brokenness does not mean we do not also reveal beauty and goodness in what we do. Our sin does not mean we do not love or serve or even demonstrate some of the highest ideals of human goodness. We do. But somehow, at the core, there is a rot, a dysfunction, an inability to make anything good last, anything pure remain, anything that is alive flourish. We all need God's grace.

The story of the Scripture, as it rolls out, reveals not only the truth of the human condition as fractured and distraught, but also the faithful work of God to restore that which was broken, to forgive us our sin and to bring about a re-creation of his broken world and shattered images.

That's the story of the calling of Abraham and the people of Israel, culminating in the coming of the One for all—all Israel, yes, but all people and all creation. Jesus came to set things right by becoming, in himself, all that was wrong, and then defeating the anger, the death, the rebellion, and the brokenness in his own life, death, and resurrection (2 Cor 5:21). Jesus hit the target we couldn't hit, every time, never sinning once—and he did it for us. It's like after a flawless day at the gun range, Jesus hands us his target replete with only bull's eyes, and says, "Go ahead and mark these scores down under your name."

And then, so astonishingly, Jesus turns to the very people who made the mess in the first place and offered us a way, not only back home, but a way to make things right alongside him. Jesus calls us into his project of grace, his mission of restoration. We become ambassadors of his grace, offering to others the grace we have received (2 Cor 5:18).

Have I gotten too theological here? It's the story we are all part of and makes sense of why we would even try to influence others in the first place. As followers of the Jesus who rescued us, we want to bring his healing and grace and life where there has been hurt and judgment and death. And we do that by being for others what Christ has been for us—forgiving, grace-filled, open, and restorative.

But it does start with our need for grace. It can't start anywhere else. Have I experienced God's grace? Am I sure of his unconditional love for me? And am I allowing his grace to cover my failure? Do I really get just how relentlessly Jesus pursues me?

Practically speaking, what I mean is this: have I bought into this idea, this ever-so-subtle yet oh-so-common idea that yes, Jesus died for me and showed me his grace before, *but if I fail now*, Jesus will give up on me. Or, conversely, have I begun to view myself through a lens that says I no longer need grace, that I am now beyond it? Do I still believe I need God's grace, every day—that without God's grace, I am in deep trouble, as well as all those around me?

Unless I am honest about my own need for grace, which connects to my integrity and transparency, then I will not be very graceful toward others. Unless I remember, daily, how Christ accepted me, then I will struggle to accept others in the same way.

As the Apostle Paul challenged us, we are to "accept one another, then, just as Christ accepted you, in order to bring praise to God" (Romans 15:7 NIV). And how has Christ accepted me? With open arms, with warmth and grace, with kindness, with forgiveness, with a vision for my life, with a call to live whole and holy, with a clear, consistent reminder of who I am and who I am becoming, which is greater than my sin, my failure, and my brokenness.

Jesus keeps calling me to follow him, not in mean or harsh ways, but with kindness. He deeply, deeply loves me and longs to see me flourish and become all he has created me to be. And he keeps extending his grace and his call to me, no matter how often I fall, fail, or fumble. While I strive to follow faithfully, I must allow failure within myself, remembering God's grace to me.

And I must allow others to fail, too. There's an old saying that I've always disliked: "But by the grace of God, there go I." I've disliked it because I felt it smacked of self-righteous judgement, as in "wow, that woman is a hot mess, but... but by the grace of God, there go I." In other words, "am I ever thankful God has been good to me and I'm not like that." That subtle judgmentalism is not helping us grow in grace.

However, there is truth in there as well, if we can watch our hearts. "But by the grace of God, there go I," if used to remember that we are all a hot mess, that we are all sinners in need of grace (and not just way back when, but right now in this moment), and when we can see others the way Jesus sees us, and offer grace to others just as we have been offered grace from Jesus, then perhaps we can use that phrase with benefit.

For myself, I remember how painfully self-righteous I was as a young man, how everything seemed clear to me, how the Bible spoke without equivocation, how other people seemed so compromised and so muddled, and I so clear. Remembering that helps me now.

Now, when I meet a young man who seems tremendously confident in his ideas, theology, and faith, I see something of my younger self. And though there's a part of me that wants to crush him a bit (just a little), I remind myself of the grace Jesus showed me, as well as the grace other mature men and women of God showed to me, and I try to extend that grace to him, as well as speaking loving truth into his life. I remind myself that he, too, is on a journey, and if I am not willing to get in close, then I will never be part of that journey, will never be able to be a helpful, maturing influence on his thoughts, life, theology, and faith.

A friend of mine at a Christian university was stunned during a student chapel to hear a young man confidently preach a deeply fundamentalist theology which marginalized women, a theology that was not only out of sync with the broader evangelical context of the school but had nothing to do with the stated theme or purpose of the chapel itself. This young man felt that the time was right to seize the platform and make a difference in everyone's lives by setting them all straight.

Of course, he failed in his objective to influence others —no one was moved by him. In fact, they were mostly upset with his arrogance and disregard for what was going on. Now, the temptation at that point was to shove him off to the side, harshly smacking him down and making him feel like he was no longer welcome anymore because of what he had done.

I don't know this young man, as I am far away from this school. But as I mused on the event in conversation with my friend, I realized how much I was like that young man at one point in my life. Maybe I would have spoken out on a different issue, but I would have been just as arrogant and confident to have seized the moment, however inappropriately, to make my views known on a topic of my passion. I would have done so in an attempt to be faithful, however misguided and immature.

Reflecting on that, I found myself hoping that there were wise and graceful people in his life who would gently and lovingly speak truth into his life, with a vision bigger than his own for what he could become.

Later I was able to speak to the chaplain of that university, and yes, there are people walking with him. You see, this is a young man with such passion and a desire for truth. And a willingness to be awkward about it, and bold enough to speak. Yes, he needs to mature, to grow, and to go deeper.

But let's not miss what's there and show grace enough to stay in the relationship and influence him toward all that God has for him. If people hadn't done that for me, where would I be? If Jesus hadn't extended his grace to me, who would I be? I'm glad this young man has people around him who choose to lean in and influence, not walk away and ignore.

Without grace, we are left only with judgment. And judgment muddies, if not eliminates, our relationships. I say "muddies" because I'm aware of how our lack of grace may not eliminate the relationship altogether, as in, for example, family situations where our kids are still living with us or we are still married to our spouse or continue to have workmates.

But the more judgmental we become, people either reject us and the relationship is strained, leading to lesser influence, or they start making decisions just because they don't want to upset us or because they want to please us, which is not the kind of influence we want.

Just as we hope will be true when we mess up, we must be willing to allow people to fail or we will not be around to influence them when they pick themselves up and move forward. Does that mean we do not speak the truth to them about poor decisions or sinful choices? Does that mean we never challenge people on positions that we believe are wrong? No, it doesn't. But we must do so with grace. We must do that in hope.

Having grace is not incongruent with boundaries or expectations; we can't grow without them. Rather, grace means that we are letting the Holy Spirit work his grace into our lives, so that we are, in turn, grace-filled for others. We strive to be always open, always forgiving, always kind, even when that seems impossible. We are willing to stay close, willing to try again, not harsh or judgmental, even when we want to run away. We refuse to write people off because Jesus refused to write us off. We will not give up on people, even when their positions or decisions have deeply offended us. And when we mess up in this, failing to give the grace we want to, we keep coming back to the heart of Jesus for us, asking him for his strength and grace for others.

Furthermore, acting upon the Scriptural advice Paul gives in Galatians 6, we seek to restore others with full awareness that the next time, it could be us in need of grace. We read, "Brothers and sisters, if someone is caught in a sin, you who live by the Spirit should restore that person gently. But watch yourselves, or you also may be tempted" (Galatians 6:1 NIV). We don't restore others harshly or pridefully, but gently and humbly, fully aware of just how much we all need God's grace and each other's help, to keep following Jesus and living by the Spirit.

There are many stories from the Bible that illustrate this grace-filled compassion, but I think the one that hits me the most is Jesus' restoration of Peter at the end of John's gospel. Peter, after three years as one of Jesus' closest and most trusted disciples, famously failed Jesus right when he was most needed. What a disappointment Peter was. How hurtful his vehement denials must have been to Jesus.

Fast-forward through that dark night and through the darkest Friday, on through that glorious Sunday morning and into the weeks that followed Jesus' unexpected resurrection. We are lounging at the seaside, and there's fresh fish cooking on the fire. Jesus is there, and so are the remaining disciples.

And Peter—eager Peter, ashamed Peter, lost Peter—he's there, too, though perhaps hanging back, unsure and feeling wretched. What would Jesus say to him? How would he treat him? Would he bring up what happened and ask why? Would Peter see accusation in his eyes? Would Jesus force him to answer for his unfaithfulness in front of the guys, rub it in a bit to make sure he's really remorseful? What was Jesus going to do?

And Jesus, so graciously, so lovingly, so kindly, doesn't ignore Peter, but nor does he gloss over the glaringly obvious elephant around the breakfast fire. Peter, who had so vocally pledged his faithfulness unto death, had faltered when questioned by a lowly servant girl. And Jesus, knowing Peter's heart perfectly, asks him one, simple question, a question that rings out over the centuries to every faithless disciple in need of restoration.

"Simon son of John, do you love me more than these?"

"Yes, Lord," Peter replied, "you know I love you."

"Then feed my lambs," Jesus told him (John 21:15 NLT).

What a question! Do you *love* me? Not "are you truly sorry?" Not "how could you, Peter?" Not "do you promise to do better next time?" Not even "aren't you going ask for my forgiveness?" None of that. Just a simple, life-changing, grace-infused question which goes right to Peter's very heart: Do you love me?

And Peter is able to respond with all his broken heart, "Yes, Lord, you know I love you." Gone is the bravado and the bluster. No more overstatements. No longer self-assured. "Lord, you know."

And following up on that affirmation of love, Peter is then given a mission: to feed Jesus' sheep and to lead his followers. And I think that's the most amazing part, because it's one thing for Jesus to let Peter back into friendship, to let him reaffirm his love for Jesus—but it's an entire other thing to then re-entrust him with leadership in the mission, to call him, only days after failing so tragically, into responsibility over others. Grace not only restores—it empowers. That, my friends, is influence.

Jesus comes back to this question and call two more times. Three times total, Jesus asks Peter to reaffirm his love, each one matching his three denials from that fateful night. Jesus does not shame Peter, but neither does he ignore his need to be restored, in the presence of his own community. And he calls him back from shame and brokenness into relationship, not only with him but now with all of his followers. Do you love me? Then, from that place of love, lead. From that position of grace, feed the sheep I love.

How We Can Grow in Grace

So, if grace is essential to our influence, how do I grow in grace? Here are five ways forward.

First, we need to start with the basics, which for me is always Jesus. Watching the way Jesus treated people, people who were very different from him, people who did not "make the grade" according to many of his religious contemporaries, shows me how to lead with grace.

And more than just his actions, the teachings of Jesus force me to dive deep into my own heart and get real about my own pride, my own cesspool of ugliness and judgmentalism, and my own propensity to put myself above others and crush anyone who opposes me.

If I am to learn grace, there is no one better to learn from than the person and the teachings of Jesus. Simple start? Pick up one of the four biographies of Jesus—Matthew, Mark, Luke, or John. Spend a few months watching how Jesus treats people, even how he talks to them and about them. And keep coming back to these gospels. Remain rooted in the story and teachings of Jesus, so that as the Spirit works these stories into your core, your life begins to emulate his grace.

Related to that, I need to embrace deeply my own need for grace. The fact is, it is so easy for us to focus on the failings of others, even on the need for us to show grace to others, that we forget how much we need grace, too. Oh, perhaps you don't need it in the same areas I do. You could be strong or mature or competent in places I am weak or immature or useless.

But, as we discussed in our chapter on humility, it is often when we feel the best about ourselves and our abilities that we are most at risk for developing a serious case of spiritual pride, which is far more noxious and deadlier than any other failure or sin. I need grace. I need it every moment of every day, and I need to remember that, grateful to God for his grace to me, and viewing others through the same lens as I view myself: a person for whom grace is essential.

Third, I must continue to grow in empathy for others. I'm circling back to previous chapters because, founded upon God's grace for us, nothing builds our practical grace for others more than cultivating empathy. Knowing someone's backstory helps me give more grace today. We need to keep leaning in, loving and listening to the heartbeat and the hurts, the stories and the struggles. We will be much less prone to judge the more we understand each other's stories.

And, fourth, we must practice kindness always. If there is anything we must remember, it is kindness. "Be kind and compassionate" becomes actionable in our daily kindness to others. If we could school ourselves in kindness—that no matter who, no matter where, no matter what's going on, regardless of contrary beliefs or convictions or actions, that we were always kind? I believe that we would grow in grace through that. There is something about habits of kindness, coupled with empathy and a growing knowledge of our own need for grace, that will enhance our relationships and expand our influence. Be kind.

And, finally, learn to celebrate small steps. We will cover this more when we get to the chapter on vision but being gracious means that we are eager to cheer people on when they make a small step in the right direction. When people begin to make healthy choices, begin to take ownership for their struggle rather than blame others, start seeing the presence of God in their daily relationships, we celebrate! Small steps can lead to big gains, and when we are encouraging growth and leading change, all steps in the right direction lead toward the goal of human flourishing.

The old hymn reminds us that "grace is greater than all our sin." And when it comes to influencing others, grace must be greater than our temptation to give up or walk away. For it is only through grace that we will become the influencers people need, helping them become all that God has created them to be.

Reflection Questions

- What does grace mean to you personally? What does it mean to receive grace from someone else?
- How does our experience of God's grace for us shape our practice of giving grace to others?
- Next time you are tempted to write someone off, how will you respond differently?
- How does studying the life of Jesus help us grow in our practice of grace?
- In what relationship are you feeling the least gracious? How will you approach that relationship with more grace now?

7

LOVE

If I... do not have love, I am nothing.
- 1 Corinthians 13:2 NIV

In the movie *Gran Torino*, Clint Eastwood's character Walt Kowalsky is a bitter, prejudiced man. And he's not happy about the ethnic changes in his neighbourhood since the days he served in Vietnam. People for whom he has no respect have become his next-door neighbours, and he wants nothing to do with them.

When a young Asian man tries to steal his beloved Gran Torino, however, Walt tries to reform him. Though there is a heart buried deep within the rough, Walt is insulting, rude, and racist, alienating everyone around him. Except the very people he hates the most: his Hmong neighbours.

Seemingly immune to his rude rejection, they are relentless in showing him grace, demonstrating kindness to him in very practical ways. They bring him food, which he does not eat. They offer help, which he does not want. And yet, as they continue to show up, to show love, Walt begins to change. Their loving hospitality, even in the face of vile rejection and insults, softens Walt's heart in a way that takes him by surprise, leading him to act in ways no one ever would have expected. Love won him over.

Love is critical to our influence. We cannot influence people in the ways we should if we do not love them as we should. In many ways, this chapter on love sits at the heart of the whole book.

When we step back and consider our influence in other's lives, we must ask the why question: Why do we even want to influence others in any way at all? And while we may point to our desire to bring good change to the world, righting wrongs and helping create peaceful and gracious communities, all of our ideals will collapse if we are not actually motivated by love for people, in particular, love for the very people we are trying to influence.

The other characteristics of influence outlined in this book are must-haves—we cannot influence effectively without knowledge, without integrity, or without respect. But love? Well, it's not just that we can't effectively influence without love—it's that we shouldn't even try.

Without love, our influence becomes manipulative, self-serving, even demonic. Without love, we begin to see people as means to the end, even if that end (we think) is somehow connected to the good of people. How many tyrannical regimes have used the "good" of future generations to justify their destruction of the living generations among them? Without love, any influence we exert quickly turns to ashes, the ashes of the people we are trying to persuade.

Love, then, is our *modus operandi*, our way of influencing others. We love people before we offer any kind of correction, before we attempt to set up supports for them, before we try to step in and change what's been happening, before we even offer our opinion. We love, first and foremost and without reservation. Love, then, determines what we say and how we say it, what we do and how we do it. Love is our motivation.

I understand that this may sound like a lofty ideal. What does it mean on the ground? I was in a coffee shop recently, and I bumped into a friend having a latte with someone I didn't know. After shaking hands, this unknown person utters something with which I strongly disagree. What do I do? I don't know this person. I don't love them. Do I just remain silent? Well, of course, sometimes that is an option we should take. Do I speak up? I'm stuck. How can I respond in love to person I don't even know? Is acting in love even possible here?

I think it is. I don't think checking our love requires a great deal of time and thought, if we've prepared ourselves in advance. It does require intentionality, however; adopting a loving posture toward people in general which then allows us to let it come to life toward each person in particular, be that the person in front of us or through the screen from us.

When we have cultivated love as our influence motivator, then we will be able to respond, even in dicey and difficult conversations, for the good and benefit of the other. Instead of responding from my angst or anger, I can respond from a desire to see that person grow. Instead of reacting out of my own need to be right and to let the room know I'm right, I can calmly begin probing with questions not designed to make me look good, but to help this other person consider better ways of thinking or responding.

Love becomes our platform, our oxygen, our stance. Far from being idealistic, this is a very realistic posture, for it assumes that I will daily interact with people who disagree with me, with whom I find very little commonality, with whom I will find it difficult to see eye-to-eye.

Armed with that realistic knowledge, I then enter a room or a conversation online knowing that I will be acting in love toward those with whom I have nothing to do. That day in the coffee shop, I opted to make a simple observation followed by question: *I can see there's more of a story behind that comment! Would you like to tell me more?* Not perfect but holding out a way to move forward in relationship.

It's easy to imagine our need for love when it comes to influencing those we really do love in the first place—our own kids, our friends, even our neighbours. What is harder is accepting our need to love the stranger, with whom we have no connection, or our enemies, with whom we know we disagree, or with whom we have even had negative and hurtful interactions. And I think that's where Jesus' teaching and example comes in.

In the Sermon on the Mount, Jesus taught his followers to embrace a new way of interacting with those who rejected, hurt, abused, and oppressed them. In other words, people hard to think well of, act kindly toward, or love. And what did Jesus say? Instead of using force to repel the person who comes against us, Jesus taught us not to resist an evildoer. Jesus taught us to act in love toward the ones who attempt to use and abuse, absorbing that abuse and then adding love to the mix.

What does that look like? Turning the other cheek,

going the extra mile, and giving away your extra coat are the classic examples Jesus uses in Matthew 5. We are not to do such things because we think the person is acting justly, but in order to love beyond the common measure and reveal true grace to a person trapped in abuse and oppression. (How this is applied can vary. It has sometimes been wrongly applied to keep women in situations of domestic violence. In those cases, "not resisting the evildoer" also means leaving the abuser, not allowing him to keep on abusing. If that's you, please hear me: you cannot help by staying.)

As Walter Wink and others have argued, pushing the oppressor to the point at which their ugly lack of love and justice may be finally revealed to them, compelling them to repent and change—that, too, is loving. Jesus then puts a very fine point on it: overturning the cultural norm, both then and now, he called us not to love our neighbour and hate our enemy, but to love our enemy and pray for those who persecute us, so that through our loving actions and loving prayers, the goodness of our Father to all is revealed through our goodness to them (Matthew 5:43-45).

And Jesus practiced what he preached, for it was upon the cruel cross that he publicly prayed for the Father's forgiveness for those who unjustly mocked and murdered him. At a time of great pain and persecution, Jesus loved his own enemies.

In fact, as we understand theologically, he died not simply by their hands, but for their sakes, dying to defeat the very death they both caused and deserved, opening up a way for his own enemies to come back to the Father who loved them. "While we were still sinners, Christ died for us" (Romans 5:8b NIV).

And we can see the way Jesus' example and teaching rippled out, so that Christians down through the centuries have gone to their deaths praying for the salvation of their persecutors, oppressors, and enemies. It is that loving stance, we discover, that is profoundly influential.

Loving those we influence is grounded in our postures of empathy, respect, and grace. But more than just grounded in them, love is their true source, for without love, all empathy, respect and grace would be hollow. Or, as the Apostle Paul poetically described, without love, the others are nothing. Remember the love chapter?

> *If I speak in the tongues of men or of angels, but do not have love, I am only a resounding gong or a clanging cymbal. If I have the gift of prophecy and can fathom all mysteries and all knowledge, and if I have a faith that can move mountains, but do not have love, I am nothing. If I give all I possess to the poor and give over my body to hardship that I may boast, but do not have love, I gain nothing. Love is patient, love is kind. It does not envy, it does not boast, it is not proud. It does not dishonor others, it is not self-seeking, it is not easily angered, it keeps no record of wrongs. Love does not delight in evil but rejoices with the truth. It always protects, always trusts, always hopes, always perseveres. Love never fails (1 Corinthians 13:1-8a NIV).*

These few verses explore the basis of all our influence. We must embrace the fact that all influence, without love, is nothing, or even worse than nothing. Without love, influence becomes dangerous. But with love, infused by love and guided by love, influence gives life, as the qualities of love are replicated in our character, attitudes, and actions towards others.

If you take what we've heard so far about influence, you will see how love is the basis of it all, for just as love does not dishonor others, good influencers show respect. Just as love is not self-seeking, healthy influencers emulate humility. Just as love rejoices in the truth, always protecting and trusting and hoping, so, too, godly influencers are empathetic. Knowledge serves others in love, not puffing itself up. Can you see the other connections? All our influence is grounded in our love, which is, in turn, shaped by the love of Jesus for us and in us by his Spirit.

Four Questions for Evaluating Our Love for Others

In order to be proactive about love, there are four evaluation questions which help reveal the extent to which our influence of others is shaped by our love for them. By asking these questions, we will be more equipped to identify ways we have been influencing from a position other than love and invite the Holy Spirit's correction in us. Through that, we'll see our influence grow as our love grows.

The first evaluation question we must ask is paramount: why do I want to influence them? We start with our motivation. Initially, our desire to influence may be reflexive, feeling only like an urge to speak up in reaction to a statement. Or it may be a longer-term plan to bring change to our workplace or instill a new habit in our family life.

Whatever the change we want to make, asking this foundational question is crucial because it helps us discern our motivation. This is a question we often fail to ask, and unchecked motivations derail good influence. So, is this change, suggestion, or statement, is it for me? Is this urge to speak or attempt to bring change for my good and for my agenda? Or is it truly for the good of all involved (including yourself) and for the glory of God?

A stark example is in parenting: it is so easy to react or to respond to our kids with our own advantages in mind, forgetting the child's needs. How many times have we tried to shut down our kids when they start getting awkward in public? How about when we use shame, threats, or rewards to push our child to perform well or accept something they don't want, all because their failure makes us look bad? It's a real challenge, but we need to ask the difficult question, "Who am I trying to make look good in this situation? Who am I trying to serve?" More than we like to admit, it is ourselves, and not our children, who occupy center stage.

Another place where it's important to check motivation is in our work. Are we making changes to the staff schedule or billing policy or daily workflow for the sake of serving others and serving those we work with? Or are we motivated by how it all serves us, elevates us, or makes life easier for us? Now, good changes at work should help both others and you, but what is driving your actions? Why do you want to influence them in that direction? All the people who are influenced by you, from your toddlers to your task managers, are begging you to get clear about your motivation, and to make that motivation love.

The second evaluation question we must ask is this: do I desire their true good? This question expands upon motivation by asking what it is that we most hope would happen for the others we are influencing.

When asked about what we desire, we often want only

the smallest of things for others. Maybe we want our preteen to eat all their food at supper, our husband to engage the kids more, or our boss to show more openness to new ideas. We set the bar too low, and we need to raise our vision for those we are trying to influence.

This vision is so important that we'll be exploring further in our chapter on perspective (chapter eight), but for now we must remind ourselves that we have greater hopes than just some mediocre change. When I lean into a difficult conversation with a friend, am I only hoping they will stop sniping at their spouse because I'm tired of hearing about it, or do I desire good and holy and beautiful things for their marriage? When I initiate a conversation with my daughter around her dependence upon social media, do I simply want her to get off her phone, or am I concerned with a more holistic vision of her well-being, safety, and knowledge of God's love for her, which I feel her reliance upon social platforms is in danger of harming?

Whenever we are trying to influence others, remember to ask: Am I influencing them with their best interests at heart?

The third evaluation question is very practical: Will this be helpful? We don't want our discussion about influence to remain theoretical; we want it to meet us right where we live. And good influence, at its most basic level, is an attempt to be helpful in some way.

So, let's ask: Will what I'm doing right now help this person become more open to God, more fully human, enabling them to live with more integrity and grace? Or will my actions push them away? Maybe I've been pushing too hard, or perhaps the timing of my influence is not right. Or, quite frankly, I know that they are not ready to make the changes they most need to make.

You see, if I push change when it's not helpful, I actually harm my influence, potentially damaging opportunities to serve later. I need to at least ask if it's helpful, even though there will be times when I am not sure, and I will make mistakes. Asking this question will push you to become more aware of the other person's needs and ability to respond. Asking if it's helpful will also shape how we approach sensitive issues or bring change to things people might be resistant to experience.

And then fourth and final evaluation question: Do I care enough to sacrifice for this? Oh, it is relatively easy to speak or suggest changes, especially for the more opinionated and braver among us. It's possible to even connect those suggestions to loving motivation, acting helpfully for their good, but then not put any skin in the game. Whether we are talking about influencing a single life or a large organization, we must do more than just lob ideas or fire critiques from the sidelines—we need to be willing to suit up and play.

In my church work, it is common to receive well-meaning advice or critique on ways we should be doing things differently or better as a church. As a leader who wants to be open to truth, however difficult, I invite these conversations. Many times, the suggestions given are good, helpful, and even motivated by love.

But what often stalls out the influence this person could have or the change that could come was the person's unwillingness to be part of making that needed change. And if you aren't willing to sacrifice to see change come, then how seriously should we be taking your commitment to see growth and development occur? You can have all the good insight in the world, but if you aren't willing to get your hands dirty working out the implications of that insight, you're far less likely to affect any lasting change.

When I think of helping friends going through a hard time, much of what happens for good or ill will rise or fall upon the willingness of the people in their lives to stay connected, fighting it out in the trench, sacrificing their time and energy, praying fervently, and remaining hopeful. If I'm not willing to sacrifice, then perhaps I need to hold back from trying to exert any influence at all?

Love is central to influence. And just as we've been attempting all along, we must ask how we can grow our love for the sake of better influence. How does this kind of change happen in our hearts? How can we make sure our influence of others is being animated by our love for others? There are two key ways I believe we can grow in love.

Two Key Ways We Can Grow in Love

First, we can grow our love by praying for the very people we want to influence. Whether this is a child in your home or a person at your work, whether it is someone whom you already have a good relationship or someone you personally can't stand, prayer is the foundation of our love-growth strategy.

Prayer, when done for the person's benefit—that God would reveal himself and transform their lives—changes our hearts towards them. That child you are struggling with? She needs you to dig into prayer for her. The super-irritating co-worker you've been coming to loathe? It's hard to keep hating someone you genuinely pray for. The parent who is constantly overstepping their bounds? Pray, pray, pray. (And then speak!)

But praying into difficult situations can be tough. We aren't sure what to pray, or we don't even trust ourselves to pray without making it about the other person's faults or slipping in our own agenda for the person. How can we do that? Praying Scripture for others, in particular taking some of the prayers that the Apostle Paul prayed for his Christian friends and praying them for others, can be very helpful. Many of Paul's prayers were even offered in contexts of relational strain or difficulty. When we take these prayers, and pray them for someone, a whole new world of praying opens up to us.

I first experienced the power of praying for someone I reviled when I was a young adult. Due to unwanted events, I felt jilted and angry at a slightly older man. I was hurt, and I wanted to see this guy fail in every way possible. Can I say I hated him? I think I was getting very close—loathing disdain, loping rapidly toward hate.

I would obsess or daydream about his demise. I would imagine him stranded on the side of the road with his truck burning in the background. It was not good. The Holy Spirit eventually brought me up short. I knew my heart was wrong but didn't know what to do about the way I felt about this guy.

I'm not sure who gave me the advice or where the idea came from, but I began to pray for him, and because I couldn't think of anything to pray with authenticity, the Holy Spirit drew me to the prayers of Paul. Even though I started praying through gritted teeth, praying these prayers changed my heart.

Paul's prayers are scattered throughout his letters, and they form wonderfully rich prayers for others. Here are three of my favourites:

- *I keep asking that the God of our Lord Jesus Christ, the glorious Father, may give you the Spirit of wisdom and revelation, so that you may know him better. I pray that the eyes of your heart may be enlightened in order that you may know the hope to which he has called you, the riches of his glorious inheritance in his holy people, and his incomparably great power for us who believe* (Ephesians 1:17-19a NIV).
- *I pray that out of his glorious riches he may strengthen you with power through his Spirit in your inner being, so that Christ may dwell in your hearts through faith. And I pray that you, being rooted and established in love, may have power, together with all the Lord's holy people, to grasp how wide and long and high and deep is the love of Christ, and to know this love that surpasses knowledge—that you may be filled to the measure of all the fullness of God* (Ephesians 3:16-19 NIV).
- *And this is my prayer: that your love may abound more and more in knowledge and depth of insight, so that you may be able to discern what is best and may be pure and blameless for the day of Christ, filled with the fruit of righteousness that comes through Jesus Christ—to the glory and praise of God* (Philippians 1:9-11 NIV).

By taking these prayers of Paul, we then pray them on behalf of someone in particular, that they, for example, "may have power, together with all the Lord's holy people, to grasp how wide and long and high and deep is the love of Christ," or that they would "be able to discern what is best and may be pure and blameless for the day of Christ."

These are powerful prayers for the person you are praying for, but even more for the one doing the praying! How long can you retain ugly judgmentalism when you are praying for the eyes of someone's heart to be enlightened so they can know the hope to which Jesus has called them? We can grow our love by praying for God's perfect and loving will to be done in someone's life, that they would truly know God's love and be transformed by him.

And what a way to pray for the people in your life you really care for! Prayers like this do have an influence on the people themselves, for prayer does have spiritual impact. And they also grow our hearts toward others, be they a child, a spouse, a roommate or a friend—and even an enemy.

As we pray these prayers, the Holy Spirit drives deep into our hearts. Bits and pieces of these prayers lodge in our minds and begin to form heart prayers for others. You can summarize them and apply them to people you realize your heart needs to grow toward: someone of a different ethnicity, a person you actively avoid, a man or a woman with whom you have much disagreement. Could this be a little of what Jesus commanded when he told his own followers to "love" and to "pray for those who persecuted" them (Matthew 5:44)? Did he know that our prayers for the very people it's easiest to hate would also influence the way of our own hearts? I suspect he did. Jesus is smart like that!

The second way we can grow our love is by taking sacrificial action. It is a good and powerful act to pray for someone's life through these prayers of Paul. And that action may be all we can take for a while and it will feel pretty sacrificial!

But what makes it real is when we begin to serve the

other person in a sacrificial and loving way, to act for their benefit and to seek their interests ahead of our own, doing whatever we can to help support their growth.

We've often heard that love is a verb (in spite of its use as a noun right there!). Real love is actionable, tangible, and lived out in life. This is easier to do when we are in mutual relationship with someone, where my sacrificial service of love is matched by someone else's reciprocity. Obviously, it's harder when the sacrificial love may not be returned to the same degree or may not even be recognized at all.

Following the commands of Paul, we are to "do nothing out of selfish ambition or vain conceit. Rather, in humility value others above yourselves, not looking to your own interests but each of you to the interests of the others" (Philippians 2:3-4 NIV). We are to "have the same attitude" Jesus had, which resulted in sacrificial service to others, ending in death. And sometimes, that's what sacrificial action will look like—humbly dying to ourselves.

How can that grow our love? Won't sacrificial action just make room for more bitterness and anger in us? If it is removed from relationship and cut off from prayer, yes it can. If we interpret sacrificial action as "give them whatever they want with no boundaries or truth spoken in love," then we are sure to burn out and turn sour.

Taking sacrificial action on behalf of someone else is acting *for* them, in their best interests—it could be that the action most beneficial to them is saying "no!" And we all know, depending on the fragility of the relationship and the learned lack of boundaries, saying "no" can be very sacrificial indeed!

But acting in someone's best interest can also mean seeking to help them achieve a personal goal even if you've been struggling to connect with them in another area. It's choosing to help a neighbour with a project he's been working on, even if there's been ongoing strain over a strata dispute. It's being willing to serve a co-worker who's been difficult to work with, all the while praying for them to experience God's measureless love.

We must step out in faith, with an agenda to serve for the sake of the other, all the while praying God's will into their lives and ours. As we do that, our hearts will grow, and love will become the platform of our influence.

In a book on influence, we could be tempted to consider our actions only pragmatically. But being able to influence someone isn't good enough—we need to be the kind of people who can be trusted, people who will not use our words or position for our own agenda or benefit, but for the good of others and the glory of God. The only way to really do that is to be people who influence others from a place of self-sacrificing, God-honoring love.

We can measure the good of our influence on others by the extent of our love for others. And then, with love as our motivating power, we can truly motivate others toward God's good for them.

Reflection Questions

- When you consider our many motivations for influencing others, why must love form our core motivation? What's in danger if it doesn't?
- How can we adopt practices of love that will influence people we barely know?

- Of the four questions for evaluating our love for others, which one connects with your need the most?
- What enemy, friend, neighbour, colleague, or child are you having trouble loving, and how will praying "Paul-type" prayers help you? Who will you be praying for now?
- What is one sacrificial action you can make to help someone grow? (Think of particular people in your life.)

SECTION THREE

THREE ESSENTIAL POSTURES

Our Posture Toward the Future Determines Our Influence In the Present.

Built upon the foundation of personal growth and the indispensable qualities of care, we must adopt three essential postures for inspiring and sustaining change long-term: a bigger vision than we can imagine, an unshakeable positivity in what people can become, and the enduring patience to see it through.

8

VISION

I can only answer the question, "What am I to do?"
if I can answer the prior question,
"Of what story or stories do I find myself a part?"
- Alasdair MacIntyre

Where there is no vision, the people perish.
- Proverbs 29:18a KJV

Toward the end of three intense years of training, Jesus was getting cornered by his enemies. He knew he would soon be snatched, tried, and lynched. Try as he might to prepare his closest friends, they couldn't understand what he was talking about and persisted in the delusion of their own faithfulness. Moments away from his arrest, Jesus tells his disciples the sobering truth: "Tonight all of you will desert me..." (Matthew 26:31a NLT).

As you may know, the disciples were having none of it,

especially Peter who declared, "Even if everyone else deserts you, I will never desert you." Was that true? No, famously, it was not. And Jesus tried to warn Peter that, far from remaining faithful unto death, Peter would deny even knowing him three times before the night was over.

Convinced of the grandeur of his own unshakeability, Peter rejected Jesus' words: "No! Even if I have to die with you, I will never deny you!" And not just Peter, but all the rest of Jesus' disciples joined in the chorus of faithful promise.

Of course, Jesus was right. They all did fall away. Deserted him. Denied him. Fled weeping into the night, filled with fear and shame and disgrace. Just as Jesus knew they would. He was not surprised by it, and laid plans for their reconnection after resurrection. How? By setting up a rendezvous point beyond the bedlam and the betrayal. "Tonight all of you will desert me.... But after I have been raised from the dead, I will go ahead of you to Galilee and meet you there" (Matthew 26:31a, 32 NLT).

Jesus had a vision for their lives that was larger than they could imagine, accounting for their failure and planning for their future. And that vision was bigger than just them. Jesus had a vision for what he was going to do through them for the world. He was able to see through that dark night and into the bright and difficult days ahead, as God's vision would unfold through them, and then through others who followed them.

In order to be truly influential, we must operate within a larger vision. We are not just influencing for the sake of influence. We are leading change, encouraging growth, challenging assumptions, retraining our own hearts and minds, as well as encouraging the hearts and minds of others *because* of the greater story in which we find ourselves, the story of God's dream for our world, which incorporates his dream for our lives.

Without this larger perspective, we won't be able to influence appropriately. We won't know where our influence fits within the context of other myriad voices. We won't know what matters and what doesn't, and we could end up fighting the wrong battle for the wrong things. Without a bigger vision, we won't know what the goal is or where it's all going, nor will we have the patience or the tenacity to stick it out.

And what is the big vision? In the grandest sense, it is the reconciliation of all things in Christ Jesus (Colossians 1:20), the world God created in every way restored, with all four fundamental relationships (with God, others, creation, and ourselves) interconnected and flourishing as God intended.

God has a big vision for this world, a vision he has always had in mind, from the moment he spoke the universe into existence. And his vision was not altered or derailed by our refusal to follow him. The tragedy of his human images rejecting his leadership has brought untold sorrow into this world, but God did not waver in his plan. He dug in deep, continuing to pursue his dream for us and for our world down through the generations of his people Israel and the coming of his Son, Jesus.

In Jesus, the Father got really clear about his big vision to make the world right again, re-inaugurating his kingdom here on earth through the incarnation, life, ministry, death, resurrection, and ascension of Jesus, and then birthing a new people of the Spirit, the church as the body of Christ on earth. And this big vision, to reconcile all things back to himself in Jesus, is a vision the Father is committed to realizing fully in the future.

We are part of that vision, having received a small preview or foretaste in the coming of the Holy Spirit, and our lives are shaped by our orientation toward this vision. As quoted at the beginning of this chapter, Alasdair MacIntyre reminds us that our actions—what we are to do and how we are to act—can only be determined if we know which story we are a part of.

If we think we are part of a story that has no overarching meaning beyond personal survival, we will act accordingly. If we believe we are part of a story that is all about my own people winning regardless of the cost to others, then my ethics will follow suit. If we have bought the story that we are just consumers or just animals or just passing through, then the way we treat ourselves, others, and the earth will naturally flow from that story.

But if we know we are part of God's own story, we realize it's the story of God making his world right again through the completed work of Jesus Christ and the ongoing work of the Holy Spirit. In this story, the Holy Spirit is applying the completed work of Jesus to all of creation, giving life and breath and purpose and power to a whole new way of living.

In the largest sense, then, our vision for others must align with God's dream to see all creation reconciled to him through Jesus Christ, experiencing his full and abundant life in all four human relationships. Everything else we do or say or plan or pray must reference that overarching goal. We must evaluate all our influence by the standard of this dream, and we must focus all our energy toward its realization. God's dream shapes our influence.

But it's difficult to operate on a daily basis with that big vision in mind, isn't it? We've got to make decisions down in the dirt of the everyday, choosing when and where and how to help people move forward, challenging others to rethink their assumptions, working on our own prejudices or biases, and evaluating progress all the same.

How can we make this big vision operational? How can we intentionally link how we interact on an online forum with the grand reconciliation of all things? Are we able to move from this big vision to a conversation with a child or neighbour or friend? Does this big vision help us when we are experiencing conflict at church? Is it even possible to hold God's vision in our heart and mind, so that our actions flow from that vision rather than just reacting as we see fit in the moment? Yes, it is.

How We Make God's Vision Operational

The first order of business is to immerse ourselves deeply in God's big story. There are just so many alternate versions of reality competing for our attention, from political stories and cultural anthems to consumer interests and corporate goals. We are constantly bombarded by multiple narratives telling us who we are and what we should be doing as a result. In a story-saturated culture, we must anchor our imaginations in the one big story which outstrips and out-explains them all: the story of God and his world.

Being immersed in God's story requires a multi-faceted approach, involving the common worship of the gathered church, regularly receiving Scripture through our ears and eyes, engaging our world with the gospel of Jesus as our paradigmatic lens, practicing intentional "Kingdom-come" prayers, and serving in the name of Jesus.

We must deliberately drink from the fountain of God's story, so that we can better discern what we taste from all the other fountains offering us refreshment and promising life. It is only as we make God's story our operational narrative that we will be able to identify the deceptive power of any story which misaligns with or contradicts God's dream for the world. We must soak in it.

The second way we make God's big vision practical in our daily lives is to identify our main relationships of influence. As you've been reading so far, certain relationships have surfaced in your mind, again and again. But there may be others that you have not yet thought of.

My advice is simple: take an influence inventory. Make a list. Who *do* you influence? What are those relationships? You will quickly think of family, from siblings to parents to children or spouse, if you have them. You may think of a few friendships that are important, both past history and newly made.

And then go on from there to think of relationships you have at work, within a social group, in the church, throughout your community, within an online forum, and groups in which you have a voice. Extend your list to include someone you might struggle with or even ignore.

Think of the soil around your house, the air you breathe, the local initiatives that are happening in your city; consider the cultural venues, political conversations, active businesses, or specific schools in which you participate.

Include your influence on yourself—heart, mind, body, and soul. Think of your relationship with the God who made you and called you to relate to him. What else? Brainstorm any relationship, big, small, near, or far, which you have the power to effect. And make a list. You'll be surprised at how large it really is.

And then, we intentionally connect the dots. Like the children's puzzles where we trace a jumble of numbered dots, we will see a picture emerge as we begin to ask compelling questions.

What is God's dream for this person, in this relationship? What is God's vision for this city, for this church, for this child or business or family member? What is God's wish for the land around me, or the birds nesting in my front yard? We may not be able to do this for all the relationships we have at first, so choose the five most relevant ones.

Think of your most significant relationships and pose the questions: What is God's dream for them? How does his vision for their lives, as revealed in Scripture, affect the way I see them? How does God's big desire for my community affect the way I influence? Like a case study, dive into these questions. Apply them to what you might be struggling with at work, or a strain you may be experiencing in your friendships. What is God's dream for them?

It may not all come together at once, but as we deliberately and intentionally make room for these questions, having become steeped in the big story ourselves, our perspective on others will shift. We will begin to see our community or our leadership or our school mates with an eye to the larger story, and that will affect how we speak, what we initiate, what we invest in, and what we ignore.

With inventory in hand, there may be times when we need to go back and reflect, even for a few moments, on how a particular role or relationship can be nurtured in the context of God's big story.

Having immersed ourselves in God's story and intentionally connected that story with our influence inventory, we can now explore more specifically how big vision helps us become good influencers. There are four ways.

Four Ways Big Vision Informs Our Influence

First, big vision helps us maximize our influence in the context of many other influences. Just as we are constantly bombarded by alternative stories, we must remember that we are not the only influence in someone else's life, be they our co-worker, our kid, or our friend.

Of course, we can be very thankful for that, for we all need shaping from other voices and characters. For example, we are happy that there are multiple, mature voices speaking into our children's lives, people of wisdom and character who care that our kids flourish and are willing to invest in their lives.

But there are other voices, too, voices that do not seek the benefit or goodness of anyone but instead seek to distract, dissuade, or destroy the work of God in others. Some of these voices are obviously poison, but many of the more subtle and seductive voices of influence do not look overtly evil—some look not only benign but even religious and good.

And yet these stories can pull us away from our ultimate purpose, encouraging us to settle for a life lived far below God's dream for us, with reference only to ourselves, our desires, our dreams, and our comfort, ignoring our higher call to be participants in God's global, historical dream to make all things right through Christ.

When I am speaking publicly about Jesus, I constantly remind myself that the good news message I proclaim with all my heart, passion, and skill is only one of many so-called good-news messages people are hearing. Remembering that both humbles me, for I must rely on the power of the Holy Spirit to convey his truth through my faulty efforts, and drives me, for I must continually speak in such a way that God's story cuts through all the other voices, calling alternative stories into question and offering truth among the plethora of lies.

For those who are involved in relationships with youth and children, we must always remember that we are not the only voice in their lives, not even the primary voice. And as a child gets older and their peer groups become more and more influential, we become more and more aware of our shrinking real estate.

This is a sobering reminder: I cannot relinquish all the space I have in my son's lives by neglecting to spend time with them. I can't get too busy to engage them with the larger story. I need to show real interest in what they are hearing through music or YouTube, from friends or school. I need to engage with them about how following Jesus intersects with the emergence of dubstep, the commentary of Philip DeFranco, the mental illness of a fellow youth, or the latest revolution reading in social studies.

So many voices jostle for highest authority, but only one has the power to bring life and freedom and purpose. Knowing God's vision, even in part, helps us maximize our influence in reference to the other visions out there. We know that we are not the only voice, so we make sure that we are present, we focus on what matters, we remember that we are dust and humbly serve in the name of Jesus for the realization of his kingdom dream.

Second, big vision helps us embrace our influence in the flow of time. Not only does big vision set us in the context of other visions, it sets our influence in the context of history. We need to think of our impact over the long haul. We need wisdom to know how to engage and when to push and what to say and why we should back off—and keeping the big vision front and center helps with just that. Knowing the big vision helps us determine not only the "what matters" question, but more importantly the "what matters NOW" question.

To use another parenting example, I cannot make decisions today without some reference to the big picture. What matters now must be determined by what matters long term: that I have a relationship with my kids that lasts my lifetime. Knowing the long-term goal doesn't mean I don't discipline or challenge or hold my kids to account, but it does mean I am always living in reference to a larger goal —God's desire to see them flourish in all their relationships, participating with him in the reconciliation of this world and doing that in relationship with us!

What does that mean on the ground? They need to hear the big story of God, to understand their place in that, and as they grow, know that we love them, support them, and that making mistakes is normal. When they do fail, we will show grace. One of the most important questions we can ask ourselves is, "What matters the most today in light of where God wants us to be in the future?"

When we have responsibilities and influence in a community, such as a community organization or in church leadership, we are often called to make decisions. Without a larger vision that helps us know where we are going, it is difficult to know what we should be doing, and not doing, right now. Many needs demand immediate response... or do they? Without a big vision orientation, all the insistent demands for attention can seem uniform, and it's difficult to discern what is a priority. Hence, squeaky wheels get greased, and the urgent shrieks receive more attention than what may be actually important.

But, when we have a larger vision, even a multi-year vision for our church or business or organization that is aiming at God's more ultimate vision of flourishing relationships, then what to do now can become clearer. We can prioritize. We can ignore. We can put something off or choose to lean in accordingly. Influence in the now becomes clearer when placed in the context of time.

Third, big vision also helps us know where to place our influence. It's the larger vision that puts the little things in perspective. Having a bigger vision doesn't always mean you won't sweat the small stuff. In fact, some of the small stuff everyone ignores might be the very things you pay attention to because you see how much they matter.

For example, there are attitudes that shape our organizations, be they at work or church or even within friendship groups, attitudes that may seem small and harmless on a daily level but end up making or breaking relationships and poisoning culture. Biting sarcasm as standard humor, cutting corners on certain practices, or enjoying juicy gossip every coffee break could all seem relatively harmless in small doses, but measured out every day, in various ways, through every level of the organization, and you've got a huge problem. In light of the larger vision, you will exert influence on the small, seemingly inconsequential things, bringing healthy changes which will have massive impact on the community.

Let me draw in one of the most bizarre New Testament stories to illustrate this point: the death of Ananias and Sapphira in the book of Acts. By the end of Acts 4, the early church was growing as the Holy Spirit came and people were flocking to the community of the Resurrected Christ. And though there was pressure and persecution from the same religious authorities which had condemned Jesus to death, the courage of the church did not wane.

Evidence of the Spirit's presence and power was not only seen through their powerful witness, accompanied by signs and wonders, it was also seen through the compassionate care of those needy among them. In a stunning reference to God's dream for a jubilee community (Deuteronomy 15) we learn that, through the generous, sacrificial giving of God's people, this early church community cared for all those in need, so that "there were no needy people among them" (Acts 4:34a NIV).

One way this happened was through the sale of land and property. Wealthier folks liquidated assets, and then gave the proceeds to the apostles, who would then see the money distributed to those in need. Amazing evidence of God's Spirit at work in them, fulfilling his promise to make them his witnesses in Acts 1:8.

Everything in this story speaks of vitality and strength. And even though there are external threats, these early Christians are not afraid. But external threats are not the only danger—this young community would need to watch for internal threats as well.

Enter Ananias and Sapphira. Motivated by a desire to

join the generosity movement, they sold some land and gave the proceeds to the apostles. But they secretly cooked the books so that it looked like they were giving 100% of the sale proceeds to the church, when, in fact, they were holding back a percentage of the profits for themselves.

And here's the deal: holding back part of the sales was not a problem—they owned the property. The money was theirs to begin with. The issue was that this couple conspired to present their generous offering *as though it was the whole amount they had received.*

So, what happened? Peter, discerning by the Holy Spirit their shared deception, pronounced judgment and each one dropped dead in turn. I admit, it's an uncomfortable story. Why such a harsh response? How could God, this loving, gracious, compassionate God who revealed himself in Jesus as the forgiver of sinners and the welcomer of all, now respond with such decisive judgment?

I've thought long and hard on this one, and here's what I think. The early church, though strong and growing, was still tender and fragile. And a gift the size Ananias and Sapphira were giving would have raised their stature in this community. Like it or not, generosity increases influence. They would have been viewed as patrons in a society governed by patron-client relationships.

In the only other example we have, just prior to this story, a guy named Joseph (nickname: Barnabas) gave generously from the sale of his property, and he went on to become a significant influencer in the early church, responsible for releasing the Apostle Paul into ministry. Barnabas's gift was an expression of his character, of his humility and generosity and commitment to the mission of Jesus.

The Holy Spirit knew that Ananias and Sapphira represented a profound threat to the fledgling church of Jesus, and before they could infect this community with their own spirit of pride and deceit, he took them out. The big vision God had for the church, of all that it would become in and for the world, down through history, was too great to risk on a sin that many may have overlooked.

Big vision helps us know where to place our influence, which could result in us doing things others deem less important. But it's also true that big vision will give us the freedom to ignore other things, even things that others think are so critical. Big vision helps us see beyond the now and judge differently.

With big vision, we will let people try and fail, because we understand the value of empowering others and growing through failure. Big vision means we can allow for strategic changes along the way, if it helps us stay true to the vision. In the light of bigger vision, we will at times end up ignoring our organizational charts or detailed plans, encouraging honesty and inviting new ideas even when they seem threatening to the status quo.

And fourth, big vision helps us remember what matters most. There are times when we are in the middle of a conflict and we can feel things heating up. At those times, we need to pause and ask, "what am I hoping for here?" We need to recall the bigger picture so we don't get caught fighting the wrong battle.

Years ago, I heard Larry Crabb, counselor, teacher, and spiritual director, relay a story that drove this point home. Late one night, Larry got a call. On the line wept a friend who'd really messed up. In fact, he was calling Larry from the hotel where he had just had an affair. Filled with remorse, still at the scene of the sin.

Larry, in reflection with us, asked a very perceptive question, a question I've never forgotten all these years. He asked, "What is my goal for this man? Was it to get him to stop having the affair? Yes, but more than that. Was it to get him to repent and confess and work toward the healing of his marriage, if possible? Yes, but it was still more than that. Was it to get this man to a healthier place so he wouldn't do this again? Well, that would be good, but that still wasn't a big enough goal. No, all those things are important, but they were not and are not the ultimate goal. The ultimate goal is that this man would become the Spirit-filled, grace-infused, new-creation image of Jesus Christ that the Father has called him and anointed him to be, living a life of Kingdom influence for the sake of God's plan to reconcile all things to himself."

That's the big vision, to which all the other lesser goals point. And knowing that goal—that massive, overarching, all-encompassing goal—influences how we respond and correct and disciple and act, even if it is late in the evening and a friend calls from an adulterous hotel hook up.

Without this bigger vision, we can easily end up fighting the wrong battles, focusing on things of lesser importance and losing our ability to influence toward God's ultimate purposes. In my conversations with Christians about our responsibility to care for God's good earth, the topic often swings around to climate change.

And because I live in a world where many people are supported, directly or indirectly, by the oilfield industry, climate change conversations feel threatening and tense. Climate change—whether it's real or not, whether it's human-caused or not, and how we should then respond to it—has deeply personal and practical implications for an oilfield operator, whether you are way up or far down the stream of production.

Now, I firmly believe Christians need to be having these conversations, difficult or not. And economics cannot be the reason we simply avoid talking about them. Much like the 19th century Christians in the southern United States whose livelihoods were dependent upon slavery had to ask (or hear) hard questions about justice and righteousness, we must be willing to ask hard questions if we find ourselves in industries founded upon the exploitation and damage to another of God's precious resources, the planet he charged us to serve and protect (Genesis 2). Doing the right thing, as we know, isn't always easy.

But when we are in the middle of those tense conversations about God's call and commission to care for his earth, be that air, soil, water, plants, animals, and people, we must not forget the ultimate goal: moving people toward a greater participation in God's reconciling plan for the whole world, including his good creation. When set within the larger vision, my hope for our creation care conversations, tense or not, is that we will each emerge with a greater understanding and desire to participate in God's creation mandate.

Whether or not a person trusts or mistrusts the science, embraces or rejects the conclusions of this or that group (and we all seem to have our authoritative groups!), this fact remains for each and every Jesus-following, Bible-believing Christian: God said this earth was good (seven times), that this earth is his (Psalm 24), that this earth is our responsibility (Genesis 1:26), and that he expects us to reflect his goodness and his vision in the way we rule, fill, serve, and protect his good earth (Genesis 1:28; 2:15).

The Great Commission of Jesus to make known God's good news to all the world isn't just about saving souls—it's about making God's whole plan through Christ real, in and for the whole world. Furthermore, the Scripture links our sin with the earth's groaning and our redemption with its recreation (Romans 8:18-25).

At the very end of the story, we see clearly God's desire all along—to make a home among us, here on the earth he loves and has restored in Jesus (Revelation 21). However you cut it, creation care cannot be dismissed. Christians are, by definition, God's conservationists. We act in God's name and as his images, for the good of the whole earth. We do not act only for the benefit of part and then disregard the rest.

And so, to come to my main point: does it matter to me, at the end of a conversation, that a particular Christian embraces the reality of climate change? No, not really. Not everyone does. What I want for Christians is bigger than that. What I want is for Christians to take their Scriptures more seriously, embracing God's big vision for us and for his whole creation, and then working that vision into their daily decisions, their vocational choices, their consumer habits, and their active lifestyles, all based upon that larger, revealed vision. They don't have to believe in climate change to be more obedient to the Creator.

My goal, in this case, is to help people become better stewards of God's creation *where they are at,* regardless of their acceptance or rejection of climate change. I want to help them think more critically about how they are living, and to begin taking steps within their lives, whatever that means, to live into God's bigger vision and their greater call.

I've used the example of climate change because it's

such a vivid example. But what is it for you? Can you think of examples in your own life where having a bigger vision can help you know what matters? You may consider struggles in your marriage, issues in your work, or decisions about your finances. By knowing the larger vision, we can remember what matters most and not get lost in the haze.

Big vision matters, determining much of the how, the what, the when, and the where of our influence. Knowing the grandest vision God has for a person, sketched out through the Scriptures, cast up large in the person of Jesus, expressed in many of Paul's prayers, and envisioned through the Revelation of Jesus to John, we can guide our own hearts and minds, as well as the hearts and minds of others, toward what truly matters.

Reflection Questions

- In your own words, how would you describe God's big vision for the world, including both the people and the planet?
- Take an influence inventory: what are the relationships (include all four human relationships) in which we are engaged, and how do we exercise influence in all of them?
- How does big vision define our daily influence? How does it help us discern both what matters and what does not matter?
- What is one key way you can keep God's big vision operational in your everyday relationships?

9

POSITIVITY

Don't use foul or abusive language.
Let everything you say be good and helpful,
so that your words will be an encouragement
to those who hear them.
- Ephesians 4:29 NLT

"You are going to be a preacher someday," she pronounced in the church lobby. Her name was Marina and she believed in me. And God must have given her some kind of prophetic insight into who I would become, long before I had any inkling whatsoever.

I think I was around 12 when she started telling me that, with all the exuberant confidence of an indigenous, Pentecostal woman. And every six months or so, *for my whole teenage life*, she would catch me by the arm and remind me of who I was going to be someday—a preacher. I'd squirm, look at the floor, mumble "thank you," and then cruise on to hang with my friends.

But I've never forgotten that. At 15, I said yes to God's call and committed my life to full-time ministry, clueless to what that meant or how it would play out. And though the road wound around and my understanding of that call matured, this is "someday" and I am a "preacher." Marina saw something beyond my own sight, something God was growing in me, and she spoke words of inspiration and calling into my life. Was that influential? You bet it was.

Positivity is influential. It flows from our vision of what's possible (chapter 8) and is rooted in our growing attitudes and practices of empathy, respect, grace, and love (chapters 4-7). We cannot truly influence others toward life and goodness without positive inspiration. Without positivity, we cannot encourage people toward bigger vision, difficult changes, or greater sacrifice. Negativity kills a life of vision, but positivity inspires a visionary life.

Because of God's big vision for us and his world, and his commitment to see that vision realized, we are hope-filled people, not hope-less people. We believe that with God, all things *are* possible, not as a naive assumption but as a fundamental reality in which our lives are rooted. We do not live in a closed world, caught within a doom loop of never-ceasing loss and degradation. We live open to the world, open to the future, because we are open to the Creator who is still open and involved in his creation, still taking us somewhere good.

As a result, we are possibility people, opportunity people, not out of some vain illusion that life is just getting better but rooted in the firm conviction that this is our Father's world and that he is actively at work in his world to bring his healing, love, and redemption to bear on everyone and everything in Christ.

As such, we can be positive. Really and truly. And we need to be, people need us to be, this world needs us to be. We need to be people who believe in others more than they, at times, believe in themselves. We need to be the ones who hold out God's vision for others to see, for our churches to imagine, and for our world to witness—pointing to God's dream as the primary dream toward which we live and work and reach and influence, even when others cannot see it. The people in your life need you to believe in them more, not less. Without that, influence can be lost.

Because it is so easy to be negative, isn't it? We can always pick something apart, pointing out faults and failures. We can be so hard on ourselves and so condemning of others. And don't get me wrong—negativity is profoundly influential. Much like drinking poison, negativity will lead to sickness and death, not to health and life.

When leaders or parents or parishioners or employees choose negativity and cynicism, entrenching a lack of trust or perpetuating a lack of vision, it kills growth and diminishes transformation. Negativity tanks the kind of influence we want to have, the kind of influence that brings life and dreams and hopes and possibilities.

Let's go back to Jesus and his pre-denial preparation of his soon-to-bolt disciples (Matthew 26:32). Jesus was not blind or naive to dark realities; he knew what was coming, better than anyone. He was a realist about the impending darkness and denial, but he was also strangely optimistic, positive, and hopeful about the future. He did not embrace negativity; he did not rage or even berate his fickle friends.

He certainly did not give up on them nor his higher vision for them.

No, he told them the truth of what was coming, and then planned for their restoration with confidence. He believed in them and hoped for them, far and beyond what they could have imagined themselves. Oh, that we would see how he continues to do that for us! And how we can do that for others.

I hear my share of opinions about the church, as I mentioned earlier. And I receive lots of encouragement and grace and support from fellow leaders, parishioners, and community members, for which I am thankful.

But, as you can well imagine, I also hear lots of criticism, cynicism, and negativity. There are people who feel disgusted with the church and unable to engage in the community as a living organization. Sometimes this is because of past hurt and disappointment; other times it is simply where they are in their journey.

And, more often than acknowledged, cynicism towards the church stems from an unwillingness to follow Jesus and deal with personal sin. As a leader who loves people, part of the reason I continue to listen is for the sake of the person engaging me—I am hopeful that in conversation I will be able to help them move forward in their spiritual journey. I also listen because I want to grow and receiving feedback from quarters not often heard helps me with that, even if it's not always delivered in a helpful way.

But let me tell you something that is not often named: people who offer critical feedback within a positive framework have a lot more influence. When I am approached by someone with a vision for how we can grow, how we can get better, how we can reach more people, ways we can become more authentic, digging deeper into the Scripture and more courageously into our community, I'm all ears. And it's their positivity that makes all the difference.

But when someone comes with a list of things that are wrong, coupled with a cynical and dismissive attitude that tears down rather than builds up, it takes a lot of discipline for me to even listen. Negativity never inspires. Cynicism never builds. Anyone can critique, cut, and deride; but can you critique and then suggest potential new ways to approach things? Are you excited about the possibility inherent within the church, or are you disgusted with the church, remaining aloof and unconvinced of the church's central role in God's mission? Your answer to that will make or break your influence. This works itself out across every relationship we have.

I'm sure you've experienced the power of positivity over negativity. To understand that power, let's explore five ways positive confidence creates better influence than negative cynicism.

Five Ways Positive Confidence Trumps Negative Cynicism

First, positive confidence inspires people, whereas negative cynicism discourages them. Watch any child learning a new skill, like riding a bike or learning to sew. What works better: giving them positive, affirming words, or sniping in with critical, cutting remarks? It's a no-brainer.

One of my uncles struggled to learn in school and suffered under the mocking abuse of his terrible teacher. The result? He cut out of school as soon as legally possible and lived his whole life thinking he was dumber than the rest of us, a conviction proved patently false the moment you met him. Negativity discouraged him from growing in ways he could have, binding him to a life less than what he could have experienced. I've often wondered how much different his life would have been had he been under a teacher who believed the best of his students and inspired them through positive and encouraging words. Day and night, I'm sure.

Many of our greatest inspirational stories feature people who went the distance to inspire others rather than discourage them. Against all odds, a leader or a coach raised the level of what their team believed was possible. Yes, they may have challenged them, shouted at them, and railed against the things holding them back. But above all, they believed in them, holding out an impossible dream and inspiring them to go for it.

Second, those with positive confidence invest wholeheartedly, whereas people of negative cynicism hold themselves back. I've noticed that it's the positive people who get in and serve, offering to build and help and create. They invest themselves—their time, energy, heart, prayer, work, gifts, life—into people and projects worthy of them. Why? Because they believe that transformation is possible. They see potential. They have faith and trust.

And so they invest. Whereas the cynical focus on the impossible, the brokenness, or the hazards, not as realists who would then overcome them but with a negativity that keeps them holding back. They never commit, never serve, never become part of the solution.

In the years that I worked in student ministry with InterVarsity Christian Fellowship, I had the privilege of raising money for the mission; more specifically, for my own ministry budget, which included my own salary but also ministry support and expenses. Despite what you may initially think, it's an honor to sit down with people from every walk of life and invite them to invest into God's dream for the next generation. My heart beat faster when I was inspiring others with what God was doing and asking them to invest their hard-earned money into student's lives. I learned a lot from these fund-raising experiences, but two things relevant to our discussion here.

First, I could never have raised money effectively and witnessed the generous investment of others into the lives of students if I hadn't believed that the students were worth it and that by investing into them, we would see Kingdom leaders growing throughout Canadian colleges and universities. If I had been cynical about the future of student ministry, negative about the next generation, dismissive of Gen Y or Millennials or "students these days," I would never have inspired the kind of invested generosity I received during my tenure with IVCF.

But, secondly, whenever I did run across people who were already negative and cynical about students, I could never get them to invest in the ministry unless I could help them see students in a more positive light. Sometimes I could help by telling stories of life change, by naming names of students experiencing God's work in them, and by narrating the ins-and-outs of our Scripture studies and mission trips and intentional mentoring and evangelism. And when I did, I was thankful to see some begin to change their view on the next generation and then partner with us in ministry.

Those resistant to it, firm in their conviction that the

students of today were hopeless, not only would they not invest in the ministry, I didn't want them to. I wanted partners who believed in what we were doing and prayed along with their giving for the work of the Spirit among us. And it would be better if they found a place to invest where they did believe God was up to something good. Positive confidence chooses to cheer and coach and encourage, whereas negativity breeds withdrawal, hesitancy, and protectionism.

The third way positive confidence wins over negative cynicism is in the way we see reality. Positivity sees what is and then challenges us to reach for more; negativity thinks that what is summarizes all that can be. Those who are positive and encouraging can be accused of being out of touch with reality sometimes—a little too optimistic or naive.

And while there are always those who seem willfully blind to difficulty, being positive does not necessarily mean being unrealistic. In fact, both positive and negative people can accurately describe reality—the difference lies in who thinks a better future is possible and is then able to truly influence others towards that better future.

In Jim Collin's book *Good to Great,* he relays the story of a man who endured 8 years of torture in a Vietnam POW camp. Reflecting on those who survived compared to those who did not, he noticed that only survivors had both a firm grip on ugly reality and an unwavering hope that there would be better days ahead. But those who were either all positive (we'll be rescued by Christmas!) or all negative (we're all going to die—no one's ever coming) struggled to keep their minds and hearts intact.

The men who were able to envision a positive future with confidence, while also acknowledging the negative experiences of today without sinking into hopeless cynicism, they survived and emerged more whole than you'd think possible. Positivity shapes future reality, enabling us to draw lines from the present into the future, rather than accepting what is as all that life can be.

The fourth way positive confidence wins is through hope. Positivity, as an expression of love, believes and hopes all things (1 Cor 13:7), whereas negativity is cynical, thinking that believing for better and hoping for more is stupid. And wherever I've seen this negativity play out, it's devastating.

The irony is that cynical, negative people can seem wise, even insightful, to those who hear them. Their doubting reluctance and their knowing smirks can cause people to feel stupid for having hope, opting for fear rather than choosing faith. In the presence of a negative, cynical person, the positive influencer can look a bit naive and foolish.

But we are, by definition, people of hope. Right at the core of our Christian faith is the conviction that God has acted in Jesus to reverse the devastating effects of sin and restore all of creation to its intended goodness and destiny —an accomplished fact of history. And even more than that, we believe that God has poured out his Holy Spirit upon all who are willing to receive him, so that his work of new creation has already begun and is permeating the whole world, like a yeast spreading through dough (Luke 13:20-21).

This is not childish naiveté, turning a blind eye to the harshness and evil that exists. This is solid hope which sees the world in the light of God's commitment to restore, through Christ and by the Spirit, what is broken and lost. Positive confidence is rooted in hope, which builds up and keeps pursuing God's dream for others.

Fifth, those characterized by positive confidence look for the good to nurture; people with negative cynicism see only the bad to criticize. Following up on our last two points, those who are positive and those who are negative may each see both the good and the bad in situations, in people, and in organizations, but what gets the focus makes all the difference in the world.

A positive influencer can see a person's poor health and still believe in a person's healthy future, stepping in to inspire, to encourage, and to help build a plan for exercise, eating, and sleep. A negative person sees the same person, but fixates on the past patterns of laziness, junk food, and fad dieting. Whether the influence will be good or bad depends upon what gets the focus. The inspiring stories we hear of people overcoming incredible odds are usually accompanied by the story of someone else—a parent, a coach, a friend, a brother, a sister—who believed in them and encouraged them to move forward. Instead of criticizing the bad, they nurtured the good, and look what happened.

Let me tell you about Jan. She gave me permission to share this, but I've changed her name for privacy's sake. Her story inspires me. When I worked in student ministry, I mentored and led many student leaders, of various abilities and giftedness. But few had the power of personality like my friend Jan.

I met Jan early in my time with InterVarsity Christian Fellowship, and it was evident how smart and vivacious and influential she was. Deeply committed to the ministry, Jan had served as a student leader during some tough years while receiving very little support from anyone in the organization.

Jan, however, had a problem. Laid over all her gifts, her commitment, her insight, and her wit was a negativity grown large through the difficult years, and it was starting to crush everyone around her. When I leaned into that, I found a young leader super discouraged and ready to quit.

The day came when she met with me in the student lounge to tell me that her term on the student leadership team was done and she was out. She was deeply cynical about everything as she was leaving. And because she is such a force, and so wickedly smart, her negativity was difficult to argue with. She had good points and worthy gripes with the organization, from our larger staff to our own student leaders. "So," she announced, "I'm done."

But I wasn't. You see, there was something about Jan that I could see, something that I'm not sure she was even aware of. When she sat at a table with 15 people, she influenced all 15. Her gift of leadership was palpable and powerful. Now, because she'd allowed negativity and cynicism to grip her heart, this meant she could cast a pall over a room faster than a skunk in the garage. But in that, I could see her ability and giftedness, even as it had become hurtful.

I took a risk that day in the student lounge. I figured I had nothing to lose, so I started talking about what I saw in her—her gifts, her abilities, her heart, her pull, as well as her wit and insight and how she had become so devastatingly negative. I mused about the way she'd come to follow Jesus, and of how she'd been mentored, and then neglected, and how that seemed to have affected her. I pointed out what I saw God doing in us as a community, and in her specifically, and then I came down to the point.

"Jan, you have a choice, right here and now. Are you going to simply give up and walk away, letting negativity win your heart? Or are you going to use this last year to step up and serve the next generation of student leaders, leaders you invited into this mission, and support them as they lead? Are you going to be a positive influence, or a negative one? Your choice." I probably went on like that for a while, attempting to cast a vision of who she could be and the difference she could make, and then I left it with her, promising to follow up with her in a few days.

I didn't know how it would go. Jan had become pretty negative, and all through my little vision speech, she seemed incredulous and unresponsive. I wasn't sure I got through to her. Nothing could have prepared me for what came next.

A couple days later, we were all together at a student event, and Jan was there in the mix. But it was a different Jan. This Jan didn't have a sour look on her face. This Jan was smiling, and what a beautiful smile. This Jan was laughing, engaged, and helpful. This Jan was here to stay. And stay she did.

I've never seen such a dramatic attitude shift happen so fast in my life. I was a bit cautious at first, wondering how long it would last. And you know what? It not only lasted, but Jan became one of the most significant influencers in our ministry that year. By the end of the year, I invited her to consider coming on staff with us. I'm not sure who was more shocked about that. The old cynical, negative Jan? I've never seen her since.

How could that have happened? I've reflected on it and come to a few conclusions. First, in my own fumbling way, I was willing to speak the truth to her in love. I didn't duck the hard conversation. I engaged in a way that affirmed her gifts and abilities and intelligence but also called her to grow. But second, I did not focus on the negative. Though I named it, which was very important, I looked for the good in her to nurture. I believed with all my heart that, if she could overcome her cynicism, her influence would be amazing. And I think that made a huge difference. God spoke into Jan's life, altering the trajectory of her life in more ways than I can count, leading her to engage her future husband, pursue her chosen career, and serve in specific ways.

But we do need to get real about the power of negative cynicism. Because, though positive confidence wins over negative cynicism in the long run, negativity is a powerful force, assimilating many into its ranks.

As I reflected on the tension of positive confidence and negative cynicism, my mind went to the covert spy mission of Numbers 13. God had brought his newly minted people out of Egypt and through the wilderness, having received the law and the tabernacle at Mt. Sinai along the way. Now they were up against the border of the very land God had promised to their ancient forefathers, and it was time to step into that promise, making God's dream a reality.

First, Moses sends twelve spies to do a little reconnoitering. And they were told to focus on two things: military strength and agricultural production. *How hard will it be for us to take them, and how good is their land?*

And so those twelve men do just that, scouring the land from top to bottom over a forty-day period, returning with sample produce and mixed news. As you probably know already, the report on agriculture was unanimous—the promised land of God was astonishingly abundant, characterized again and again as a land "flowing with milk and honey" and illustrated by clusters of grapes requiring the strength of two men to carry.

But the military report was mixed: ten of the spies

talked of the enemy's immense size—apparently the locals didn't need two men to harvest their grapes! These ten spies emphasized the size and fortification of their towns, all the while sinking lower and lower into hopeless defeat.

Two of the spies, however—the now famous Joshua and Caleb—offered the minority report, acknowledging the same realities of size and power, but choosing instead to emphasize the faithfulness of God's promise and power. Caleb, sensing the devastating impact these ten spies were having upon the people, opted for immediate action. Speaking over their negativity, Caleb shouted: "Let's go at once to take the land. We can certainly conquer it" (Numbers 13:30 NLT)! But negativity had already won the day. Fear took hold of the hearts and minds of the people God had promised to take into this land. They rebelled and refused to go in.

When Joshua and Caleb tried to offer a positive report on the new land for God's people, their positive faith was overwhelmed by the negative fear of the ten opposing spies. Everyone saw the same thing; all experienced both the bounty of the land as well as the powerful deliverance of God from Egypt.

And yet, only two were willing to see reality and how it could change; the other ten saw reality and believed it to be the only one that existed. Who won the day? The voices of negativity, cynicism, and faith-less-ness. To the ears of the people, the negative report seemed so wise, so cautious, so right. But it left God's people wandering for forty more years. Though positivity wins though hope, negativity kills through despair.

Doesn't this example undermine the power of positivity over negativity? You have to read on to discover the full story. True, the positive confidence of Joshua and Caleb didn't end up influencing their own generation, but it did position them to influence the next. And in our lives, not everyone will believe that life can be more whole, that churches can grow, that families can flourish, that businesses can get better, and that communities can be healthier.

Some people, stuck in mindsets of the status quo, won't be able to step up into what you know can be, to embrace God's vision for the future of your church or community. But even in those times when those around you—your own peers, your own staff, your own family—won't go along with your positive confidence, know this: others will. It might be people who are outside your immediate sphere, it may be the next generation, it might be folks you didn't expect to show up.

Joshua and Caleb faced the disastrous disobedience of God's people and ended up leading them for forty years through the wilderness until the next generation—the children of their now-dead peers—were ready to get in on God's promise to them. And when it was all said and done, who was left standing to lead God's people into his dream for them? The two who believed in God's promise. All the rest died in their shrunken reality, but Joshua and Caleb led the people into God's expansive vision, confident that God's plan was irrevocable, even if it had to be delayed because of disobedience. It may take years, but positive confidence will win over negative cynicism and the results will be honoring to God and great for people.

Let's make this personal. Take a step back and ask yourself how others experience you. Would they characterize you as a person of positive confidence or negative cynicism? Is your influence winsome, based upon your thinking and your attitude? Because the way we think with our minds has significant impact on what we do with our lives, and it will shape our influence of others.

I know that positive thinking has often received a bad rap in Christian circles, deemed as just a "think it and it will be, mind-over-matter" kind of self-belief, cut off from a robust faith in God. But the Bible is replete with teaching about the power of our minds. The positive thinking, self-help genre is onto something true, and focusing on the power of our minds has helped many people break cycles of negative, deceptive thinking and experience change in their lives.

However, if positive thinking isn't rooted in the truth of who God is and who we are as his images, it can lead us to a place of greater self-sufficiency and not God-sufficiency, which, though it may make us better in some ways, could leave us less open to God, less dependent upon his grace, and less in touch with our need of his forgiveness. And that, positive though some of its results may be, is ultimately deadly to the soul.

Within the context of God's revelation though, positive thinking is incredibly powerful. Rather than fixing our hearts and minds on the lies, the junk, and the false narratives that try to define us, we choose to hold in our minds and hearts the ultimate truth of who God is and who we are. In Romans 12:1-2, we are urged, in view of God's mercy just outlined by Paul in the previous chapters, to offer our bodies as living sacrifices to God as true and proper worship, holy and pleasing to God. Then we are challenged not to be conformed to the pattern of this world, but to be transformed by the renewing of our minds.

The net effect of this mind renewal? We will be able to test and approve God's good, pleasing, and perfect will. Offering our bodies to God and being transformed by the renewing of our minds are connected to living the life God desires for us—the holy, pleasing, and good life. And our minds play a critical role. We cannot ignore what we are thinking, the kind of information we are taking in, and the influence that truth or lies has upon our life under God.

To be a person actively renewing your mind means that you have to choose what you will focus your attention upon. That does not mean you stick your head in the clouds (or the sand) and ignore the ugly truth, the broken situations, or the perpetuation of lies around you. But it does mean that you regularly fix your attention on the things that bring life, meditating upon truth that transforms.

In another of the Apostle Paul's letters—the one he wrote to the Christians in Philippi—he encouraged anxious Christians to bring all their concerns to God, translating their worry into prayer, and promising peace as a result. Then he challenges them to think strategically, because he knows that practiced worriers may take their concerns to God in prayer and still keep obsessing over the negative, difficult, and ugly things that are going on around them.

What should we do to inspire positive confidence? Paul invites us to think differently. In a very famous passage, we hear this challenge: "Finally, brothers and sisters, whatever is true, whatever is noble, whatever is right, whatever is pure, whatever is lovely, whatever is admirable—if anything is excellent or praiseworthy—think about such things. Whatever you have learned or received or heard from me, or seen in me—put it into practice. And the God of peace will be with you" (Philippians 4:8-9 NIV).

Eight Focus Areas for a Positive Mindset

We can apply this challenge to our influence. In the context of every relationship, in the situations we face as leaders or parents or employees or friends, we are faced with choices: what is going to get my attention? What will we fix our minds upon? Again, this is not about ignoring difficulty, refusing to deal with what is wrong or failing to stand up for what must change. This is about the state of our minds and the focus of our hearts. Will I be negatively cynical or positively confident?

This Philippians list provides us with an insightful set of questions. At a difficult moment in my marriage, when things are strained between co-workers, as I am upset about struggles in my organization, or when I hear something that turns my stomach, what—*at that very moment*—will become my focus? When I consider my influence on others, what will fill up my mind's attention? What we think affects how we influence. Let's go through these eight focus areas and tease out some implications.

True: Will I fix my mind on what is true? When there is tension or difficulty, truth is more important than ever. Will I focus on what is true about God's presence in this situation, true about our identity in Christ, true about this relationship even if it's currently experiencing difficulty? Will I focus on the truth of what is happening or has happened? Or will I choose to fix my mind on the easier-to-believe lies—that person never did love me, he is just an idiot, this church is full of hypocrites, I never should have tried to help them, or God has abandoned me? We always have a choice. Will we think about what is true or wallow in what is false?

Noble: Will I gravitate to the nobler things or fixate on what is shameful? Knowing how powerful shame is within our culture and within our own hearts, we may have to dramatically assert our choice to think of what is noble. We may need to name the shame that surfaces when conflicts rise or when failures occur, so that we will not be sucked into self-loathing shame but drawn toward noble thoughts. When in conflict, we must not ignore the power of shame within both ourselves and others. Good influence can be instantly derailed if shame dictates the terms of our interactions.

Right: Will I choose to look at what is right, or will I be determined to expose all the wrong I see? I'm not talking about ignoring injustice or overlooking sin and hurt—that would not be right or helpful. But how often are we so concerned with what is incorrect that we refuse to see what is right, what is going well, and what can be encouraged? Both are usually present, but which one gets my focus? When it comes to mentoring a new staff, encouraging a volunteer, or growing a ministry team, who would you rather have leading the charge: someone who is always going on about what is wrong, or someone who sees fully what's happening, but seems relentless about naming what is right?

Pure: How much will I fill my mind with the pure things rather than the ugly things that can surface so quickly? In our relationships, it's often easier to imagine others' motives in impure ways, seeing in them what we are often blind to in ourselves—self-righteousness, pride, arrogance, intractability, or indifference. And when trust has been broken and needs to be repaired, choosing to think pure thoughts about others represents an act of trusting faith, not only in God, but in others. But I can tell you this: you will not be a healthy influencer if your thoughts have been captured by impurity—that will leak out and destroy whatever good influence you could have had.

Lovely: How about the lovely things rather than the hateful ones? Make no mistake: hatred can be very motivational, driving us to defeat others and achieve more, or so we think. Even hatred toward injustice and evil that can seem so right ends up eating our souls.

A friend of mine worked on the frontlines of humanitarian crises worldwide. Within days, whole tent cities appear, fully operational, filled to overflowing with people fleeing conflict. During her time in that work, many good people were present, fighting for what was right, but not all were motivated from the same source.

Some were motivated by what was lovely, what needed to be saved or preserved or protected; others were motivated by a strong, burning hatred for what was happening, the evil that was choking the life out of others, or the perpetually insane decisions by a few who disregard the well-being of the many. And what she noticed, over time, was stark: the aid workers motivated by hatred became uglier, more difficult, and eventually burned out. It was only those sourced by love and willing to see the lovely in the mess who were able to continue serving over the long haul.

While there is a place for righteous anger and hatred against evil, it could not be at the centre of their motivation without consuming them. In her personal journey, she realized she had to have a deeper passion for the lovely than a loathing for the ugly, or she would never last. None of us could.

Admirable: As a person seeks to bring good influence

to organizations or people, there will always be actions or people or things that seem difficult to admire. Attitudes, inconsistencies, fear, and selfishness can be so harmful to our experience of God's grace. However, we must be the ones who raise the bar on consistent admiration, fixing our thoughts on ideals, on models, on Scripture, on healthy motivations, on the vision God has given us about what is admirable rather than despicable. One of the roles of positive influencers is to note the admirable, expressing publicly our admiration and leading others to see what we see.

Excellent: A significant aspect of influence is our pursuit of excellence—excellence in our relationships, our work, and our systems. Rigorously pursuing excellence does not necessarily mean fixating on perfection, though it could slip into that.

Rather, to think on what is excellent means that we aim at the best, not settling for shoddy or "good enough" when we could have achieved greater health, wholeness, and beauty. Our influence on others should inspire them toward excellence in their art, their thinking, their leadership, their self-care, their perspective, their relationships, and their work. Taken with all that we have said in this book, fixing our minds on excellence need not be oppressive or tyrannical; it calls all of us to pursue greater things together, living into the dream God has for us all.

Praiseworthy: And perhaps nothing influences more effectively than a parent or friend or leader who is always looking for an action or attitude or aspect of life that is worthy of praise. Exalting God's gracious presence and activity during difficulty, remembering to highlight good achievements in the middle of a failure, and teasing out the hidden beauty when everyone has become depressed with the ugliness—that is part of the art of influential leadership.

As we've said throughout this chapter, it is just so easy to criticize, to cut down or tear apart. And we must acknowledge reality, explore difficulty, and name what has gone wrong or taken us apart or our influence will be less compelling. But all throughout, we must not lose sight of the greater reality and the larger vision. We must maintain the positive tone set by Philippians 4:8, allowing the true, the noble, the right, the pure, the lovely, the admirable, the excellent, and the praiseworthy to garner our greatest attention, for the sake of those we love, for the sake of those we are leading, for the sake of our own hearts, and in honor of the One who is leading us all.

What a list. I'm convinced that if we spend a greater portion of our time thinking only of things that meet these criteria, our hearts and minds would not only experience greater peace, but we would begin to influence others toward greater peace as well. As good influencers, we can become people who willfully and defiantly (yes, defiantly) see the good, the best, the holy, the pure—not at the expense of truth, but in service of the greater truth. We point out the fact that there is a good God at work in this world, that we who are created in his image have been given responsibility to love and serve and change his world, and that we can help people experience greater purpose, better relationships, and a more genuine encounter with the love and grace of God. With that in our minds, how can we not be positive in our influence?

Reflection Questions

- Can you remember a time when you were inspired by negativity? How did that work for you?
- Where have you seen positivity help others grow and learn?
- Why is it difficult to invest in people and projects when we are negative or cynical?
- How can you nurture the good rather than simply criticize the bad when faced with difficult choices or relational conflict? What difference will that make?
- Of the eight focus areas for positivity gleaned from Philippians 4:8, which one is the greatest challenge for you? How can you apply these to your leadership and relationships?

10

PATIENCE

Being confident of this,
that he who began a good work in you will carry it on
to completion until the day of Christ Jesus.
- Philippians 1:6 NIV

The end of a matter is better than its beginning,
and patience is better than pride.
- Ecclesiastes 7:8 NIV

As we come to this final chapter, I want to pull it all together by exploring the one attitude that could make or break everything we've done so far. Our ability to influence others depends on our willingness to let people and organizations grow at a pace slower than we'd like. Yes, I'm talking about patience.

The old joke about praying for patience and being frustrated with God's slow response reminds me of how difficult this really is. No wonder patience is one of the fruits of the Holy Spirit (Galatians 5:22), perhaps the slowest to grow in our lives and one the Spirit must continually prune to produce.

You see, if we have a vision for some good change, we are naturally impatient to see it realized. Why would we delay? We are eager to see lives expand, organizations improve, churches grow, and families flourish. We are often thinking ahead about necessary shifts to help things grow, long before others are even aware of the need for change.

And when the daily reality of life does not yet match the dawning hope of a better future, we can be in danger of an impatience that destroys the good work that is happening today, even if it's not always as obvious and clear, and especially if it's slow. In order to affect meaningful change, however, we need to be patient enough to bring people into that future.

The Bigger the Vision, the Better the Patience

The strength of our patience is tied to the size of our vision. Does that strike you as odd? Yes, big vision can make us impatient. But I want to suggest that the ability to cultivate patience comes when we embrace God's largest vision, connecting how our patience, over time, contributes to the realization of his dream. Big vision does pull us forward (which can make us impatient), but a long-term vision also helps us stay the course, believing that more change is possible over the long-term, with patience, than anything we impatiently demand to see in short-term.

One of my greatest mentors, Alan Jones, often remarks

on his impatience to realize God's dreams for the church. Alan has served as the lead minister in the Grande Prairie Church of Christ in northern Alberta, Canada, for almost 40 years. As a teenager, Alan came to Christ through the Grande Prairie Church of Christ youth ministry. In 1983, after theological education, Alan assumed pastoral leadership there.

In the mid-90's he hired me, a young, inexperienced, barely-twenty, Bible school graduate. And while Alan likes to poke fun at himself for being so impatient and quick to flare up, he was an incredibly patient mentor. Though he'll find it odd to be offered as a positive example in a chapter on patience, Alan demonstrated the kind of patience we all need to foster.

You see, as much as Alan would get excited when things were moving too slowly, I've never met a man more willing to extend grace, time, and developmental growth to others. And it was always tied to the bigger vision. Alan (and he'll hate that I'm saying this—I didn't ask his permission) is actually a very patient leader with a long-term, bigger-than-ever vision, and it was his big vision that kept him believing in the church and investing in young leaders like myself. If it weren't for his patience, I wouldn't be where I am today.

Alan used to encourage me by leaning forward in his chair, and with his muddled Liverpool-Canadian accent, evoking this truism: "Tom, you can accomplish a whole lot less in one year than you'd hope, but way more in five years than you'd imagine."

And that was how he led, knowing that if we only think a year ahead, and then expect big changes in that time frame, we'd be impatient and frustrated, constantly. But if we'd widen the scope, lengthen the period of time, and then take intentional steps toward the vision, we'd see many more changes realized. When frustrated with the slowness of pace within the church, he loved to quote some forgotten writer who said, "Like a mighty glacier, moves the Church of God." Yep. And you can apply that to any good change, anywhere. I can't think of a greater image of power than a glacier, but, wow, they move slow.

When Frustrated with Slow Change, Check Your Heart

We often use big vision as an excuse for impatience, but it's not always as connected to the vision as we think. Yes, we can be frustrated by the slow rate of change. And yes, there are people in our families or organizations who will resist movement and make initiating good change difficult.

But what I've realized is that much of our impatience is darker than that. We may dress it up with phrases like "holy discontent" or "leadership gifting" when, in reality, we've failed to do some of the necessary work to make change possible. We can become absorbed in our own agenda and forget that we are working with real people who are living pressured lives, struggling with relationships and hurts and doubts and fears. We can forget to listen and falter in love, unempathetic and unaware of why a person or a family member or a friend may be resisting the change you are attempting to lead.

In the local church, change can be notoriously difficult to bring, especially if it's happening in a community that hasn't experienced a lot of change (other than slowly dying from visionless attrition, which though tragic, never feels dramatic and often goes unnoticed). One dynamic insight that has helped me so much is this: much of the pain expressed over change is not because of the change itself, but because of the loss that the change brings or uncovers.

In the church I lead, we have experienced sweeping changes over the last 7 years, changes that have been embraced by a community willing to grow and help people find and follow Jesus. But whenever there has been struggle with the pace or scope of change, it's been helpful to look for the loss that is being mourned, rather than assume that the feelings being expressed represent settled resistance to actual change. When loss is acknowledged, empathy is employed, and people can mourn, it's amazing how the same people can then move forward and embrace tremendous change for the sake of a bigger vision.

When I feel impatient with the slowness of change, I must also check my own heart. I need to ask myself, "Am I impatient because my agenda is being delayed?" In other words, does my impatience stem from personal frustration with people slow to do what I want them to do? It's so easy to dress up our frustration in spiritual language, with appeals to our vision, God's will, and what we've all agreed upon. (Pastors are experts at that!)

But is that what's going on? Maybe, but maybe not. Perhaps my impatience is more tied to my ego than God's glory. A gut check is paramount before I start challenging people for their resistance to change. I need to make sure I've done all I can to understand and empathize with why someone might be slow to embrace change.

I can imagine some of you feeling frustrated with what I am saying. Even now you might be thinking of "that difficult person" who resists good change. It could be your 12-year-old son, your boss at work, or your leadership board at church. But here's the truth: all is lost if we don't let people grow slower than we'd like. If we aren't willing to wait, to help, to slow down, then we will kill our good influence. Without patience, many people will simply check out, refusing to come along.

And you know what else happens when we aren't patient? People feel bullied. Too many people, particularly in churches, have been pressured by a leader, a pastor, or a parishioner into change they weren't ready to make. And I don't mean they weren't ready to make it because they were just stuck and unwilling to change. I mean they were never helped along the way, never heard, never led through a process of discovery and transition, exploring purpose and mission and then embracing the need for change that God's vision compels us to make. No, they were essentially forced to acquiesce.

As a result, they felt run over by the leadership. They felt used and abused. Pushed before they were ready, they ended up failing to support the mission and get behind the change they were unable to engage. And why? Because their leaders weren't patient enough, wouldn't slow it down, couldn't keep the larger and longer vision in mind and embrace the fact that the slowness of the pace today does not negate the power of glacial movement over time. And the real tragedy? The larger vision of a church spiritually and missionally vibrant is thwarted. People shut down, clam up, and get out; everyone (including the leader) feels disappointed and disheartened by the results.

The same is true of our personal relationships. Your friend

is resisting changes that would make a huge difference in their lives. It could be overcoming a harmful addiction, getting out of a destructive relationship, or acknowledging a real need. But they aren't ready. Oh, they say they are. They want to be, and when you are in the middle of an intense coffee chat, it's all about the right decisions and new habits and things they are going to do differently. But two days later, their vision has faded and it's same-old-same-old—that dead beat is still hanging around, that terrible habit remains firmly entrenched, that unacknowledged need is still... unacknowledged.

And you've been empathetic, you do love them dearly, and you really have offered sound, humble advice. But they aren't changing. And it's so frustrating. You can see how they are continuing to harm themselves through their lack of initiative, and you want more for them.

Now what? Well, you might do what others have tried. You could start pushing your friend to make needed changes. You might exert pressure, stepping in too far and making decisions for them, all in the name of helping and accountability. You bravely pour their stash down the drain or delete that number from their phone. You could order a healthy salad when they wanted fries or come by and start packing up your friend's stuff, so she can leave an abusive relationship.

In short, you could start pushing for changes before they are ready to make it for themselves. And that's a recipe for failure. Not only will it not work, it will put such a strain on your relationship that it might not survive. Either they will pull away from you, because you have broken boundaries and began to take even more power away from them, in the exact area they already feel powerless, or you will pull away, letting your frustration with their lack of growth to taint your heart toward them.

I've seen many people abandon friendships because "they weren't willing to do the right thing" (which usually means "what I've told them to do"). Or "they've become such a drag on me and I need to surround myself with healthy people making healthy choices."

And while there is truth there—you do need to surround yourself with people pursuing good goals and growing healthy habits—we cannot simply drop our friends because they move slower (sometimes imperceptibly so) than we'd like. Here's the truth: if you push them so hard they pull away, or if you cut ties with them because they aren't performing to your standards, you will have eliminated your influence, both now with your persistent, loving example, but even more poignantly in the future when they may finally be ready to change.

Real, lasting change doesn't happen according to my timetable; often something must shift, an event has to occur, or a person needs to experience something that finally enables them to take the steps needed for change. And if you've already left the party, you won't be able to be part of what God is doing, having abandoned your influence long ago.

Taking the Long View on Growth

If we are going to bring good influence to bear on our relationships, workplaces, churches, and organizations, we must become the kind of people with a longer-than-imagined vision to allow for slower-than-preferred change. As leaders, we must be willing to set aside our own pride and impatience, so we can invest in the people and organizations and churches we have been called to lead. We need to opt for the influence of a long marathon, not a short sprint.

When we think of the people in our lives, this means that we are willing to make longer commitments to them, rooted in God's big vision for them, and then we need to pace our influence within that longer timeframe. This means we don't give up on people who seem slower, who seem to dawdle, who resist and even reject our influence.

Oh, don't get me wrong here—I'm not talking about embracing mediocrity or ignoring someone's selfish preferences. In order to influence, we must lean into tough conversations about growth and character—we must be willing to push people and ask hard questions. We must pray fiercely and fervently for their hearts and lives.

But being patient does mean that I am not going to give up on someone who seems to be walking when we should be running, or seems content to lounge when we should be working. I will challenge them to get up, but I will not leave them behind. I will remain convinced that God's desire for them is greater than I (or they) can imagine, and I will stay connected, prioritizing my relationship with them in the hopes that there will come a time when this person will be ready to move into all that God has for them.

I need to be more okay with slow, willing to let people grow at their own pace. Applying all that we've examined so far—especially empathy, grace, love, and vision—we must take a long view of development. As people-lovers we ask, "What are the next steps for this person?" Perhaps that is clear; many times, it is not. When we think of our churches or families, we take a longer view of growth, too. And we ask ourselves this question: "What is a simple step I can take to encourage good, healthy change?"

When we think of incremental changes within the grand scope of vision, my mind always sweeps to Philippians chapter one. The Apostle Paul is writing to a community who has supported him from the first days they heard about Jesus through Paul and came to follow Jesus as the Messiah. His little letter reveals a man whose big vision was rooted in a heart of empathy, grace, and love.

Listen to this. Paul says,

I thank my God every time I remember you. In all my prayers for all of you, I always pray with joy because of your partnership in the gospel from the first day until now, being confident of this, that he who began a good work in you will carry it on to completion until the day of Christ Jesus.

It is right for me to feel this way about all of you, since I have you in my heart and, whether I am in chains or defending and confirming the gospel, all of you share in God's grace with me. God can testify how I long for all of you with the affection of Christ Jesus.

And this is my prayer: that your love may abound more and more in knowledge and depth of insight, so that you may be able to discern what is best and may be pure and blameless for the day of Christ, filled with the fruit of righteousness that comes through Jesus Christ—to the glory and praise of God (Philippians 1:3-11 NIV).

Do you hear Paul's heart for these Christians? And what's more, he's got a huge vision in mind, which he is praying into: that their "love may abound," that they "may be able to discern what is best and may be pure and blameless," and "filled with the fruit of righteousness that comes through Jesus Christ." Huge vision gives him the ability to set their current growth, their actual community, their present struggles, and their exciting success within this larger context.

And what's more? In the often-quoted verse 6, Paul is confident "that he who began a good work in you (and he's not talking about himself!) will carry it on to completion until the day of Christ Jesus." Paul's confidence in their transformation is rooted in God's faithfulness to finish what he's started, to carry through on what he's initiated, which goes way beyond his own influence and ability and life-span. This is the confidence of a leader who understands his place within God's plan, who knows the importance of his influence and yet does not inflate that importance beyond its proper range, entrusting the full and final vision to God himself.

As I've walked with people experiencing God-sized change in their lives, I've had to hold on to this confidence, often with both hands. And it's helped me become more patient and grace-filled as well as less anxious and demanding. Confident that God is at work, I can relax and be gentler in my leadership.

A few years ago, a young couple began connecting with our church. Neither were from churched backgrounds, and neither were following Jesus. Unmarried, they had two delightful children, and they found a home in our church.

He came first, and with an intensity unmatched by most. He would awkwardly hover, and then rapidly engage me with spiritual questions. Brow deeply furrowed, he would lob his wrestling thoughts out and wait for my response. Finding out that he was not alone in life, I encouraged him to bring his family. And within a few months, all four had plugged in. The kids loved the children's ministry, and both the mom and the dad began to feel God's Spirit calling them to come.

But it was slow going. There was lots of struggle, personally, relationally, and spiritually. It was months of push and pull. They would respond, then resist, then respond some more. And yet it was so evident that God was at work.

Over the next year and a half, this family was simply loved into God's family, each one taking steps appropriate to where they were at. They were encouraged to serve, and they started contributing to the ministry of the church in ways that fit their spiritual journey. And wow, were they growing!

In conversations both intense and invigorating, this man and this woman started expressing their desire to follow Jesus. They knew Jesus was calling them to follow, and they wanted to give their lives to him. It felt complex; their hearts were conflicted, and their lives were complicated.

You see, even though they wanted to follow Jesus, they didn't know if they wanted to stay together as a couple. Did "getting married" to Jesus mean getting married to each other? They weren't sure.

Convinced that God was firmly calling them, they were baptized into Christ, but still unsure of their future together. And, convinced as I was of God's work in them, I encouraged them to say yes to Jesus and then let Jesus help them sort out their future.

Some would criticize that decision—I baptized into faith an unmarried couple who were still unsure if they wanted to be married. And yet, how else were they to come? We don't clean up our lives so we can come to Jesus—we come to Jesus and then let him clean up our lives. Which he does. Though often more slowly than we like.

On the outside, it may have looked like this couple didn't realize Jesus might want to make some changes in their relationship. But they knew. And (unknown by virtually everyone) as an expression of their love for Jesus and their desire to honor him with their lives, they even slept separately while maintaining a household together.

And they sought Jesus' direction for their lives. Should they overcome their fears and doubts and covenant together in marriage under God? Or should they call it quits and formally separate, knowing how tragic that would be for their kids? It was a long, arduous journey to the altar. But yes, there did come a day (in no way a foregone result, however this story may sound) when they stood before witnesses and pledged their lives to each other under God, uniting in holy marriage what had only been a common agreement. And the journey of growth and transfåormation continues. What a delight this family is, and what a testimony to the work of God which transcends our own timetables.

When I reflect on this story, I remember how anxious I was, at times, wondering if I was being a little too patient, a little too graceful, allowing for a little too much time to process Jesus' leadership in their lives. But that anxiety was all about me, wasn't it? Jesus wasn't anxious in the slightest. He never is. He was present to them, he was working in them, and he was thrilled with each faltering step after him.

And he was patient! Here's the relevant question: what would have happened if I'd been too impatient to wait for them? What if I'd pushed them to make a decision before they were ready? What if I'd put my own timeline on their journey, rather than letting God move them at the pace he knew they needed? I shudder to think of how devastating that could have been for them, and for us.

God's Powerful Patience

True influencers remember the big picture, patiently confident in God's faithful work. Being patient is not code for silence or an excuse to avoid confronting people with difficult truth. Being patient doesn't mean we never push.

Being patient means that we submit our own time frame for making things happen to God's longer will and timing. We remain attentive to the work God is doing, the signs of life as they come, the hidden and deep activity of the Spirit beneath the soil, and we measure our actions accordingly.

It's difficult to think of a Biblical story that doesn't showcase God's patience with people. From the very beginning, when humans failed to follow God's loving leadership, he stepped in to cover their shame and initiate a very long-term rescue plan. Even there in the Garden of Eden, God points towards Jesus' coming to restore what was broken and crush the serpent's deceiving head (Genesis 3:15).

God was patient—achingly so—with his plans to give a child to Abraham and Sarah. He seemed in no hurry at all when his people went down to Egypt, even though he'd already committed a special country to Abraham, Isaac, and Jacob.

Hundreds of years later we see God's patience with his own frail people, working to bring them out of Egypt and into the Promised Land. And then down through the story, as God's people would cycle through faithfulness and unfaithfulness, God is patient. All the while moving his story towards his climax in the coming of his own Son Jesus, fulfilling his dream for Israel, and restoring life to his precious creation.

And look at the life of Jesus! For 18 years (12-30 years old), Jesus built things—fixed doors and covered roofs and assembled benches. Eighteen years! And then he ministered for just three before going to the cross. We already discussed how Jesus patiently called his disciples to keep following him, through the darkness of that last night and beyond to resurrection.

Wait, you say. Haven't I glossed over the times when God came down in judgment, as he did at the flood, upon Egypt, even upon his own wandering children in the wilderness of Sinai? How about when Israel was dragged off into exile by one foreign power, and then returned to the land only to struggle under the oppressive thumb of another one? And what about Ananias and Sapphira struck dead in Acts 5? What about that?

God's patience is seen every step of the way, both in how he waited and allowed people time to change, to repent, and to listen, but also in how he worked to bring his whole people to full restoration, acting at times in judgment so that more people could receive new life in Christ.

The Lord of history, with the longest possible view, is incredibly patient with his slow people. He truly will, as Paul said in Philippians 1:6, carry on to completion the good work he started in us.

In my own life, God has been very patient with me. I've been slow to come around to his way of thinking. I've resisted his will in my life. I've hindered the work of the Holy Spirit and grieved him with my selfishness. I've persisted in my own ways, and only come around to God's way when other options have failed. I've mistrusted him when he's the only one fully worthy of trust. I've willfully forgotten his promises to me and sought solace in my own plans.

And guess what? God patiently works in me anyway. My spiritual growth can be measured like a day-traded stock, spiking up, then dipping down, and all that before noon. God steps in, nudges me a little, maybe applies some pressure, sends someone to challenge me, then steps back, waiting for me to respond. Patient, patient, *patient*—far more patient than I will ever be. And I am so thankful, for it is his patience and his kindness that wins me over, giving me opportunities to grow, to repent, to change, and to invite his work more deeply in my life.

And so it is the God who is so patient with me who then calls me to be patient with others. The leadership of Jesus in my life is a model for how I must relate to others. As Jesus has accepted me, I must accept others. As Jesus has forgiven me, I must also forgive. As the Father is kind, as the Spirit is supportive, as the Son is oh so gracious, I must be the same for others. For it is only as I am for others what God has been for me that I will be able to help others move toward all that God has for them, however slowly that journey may be.

In order be a good influence for others, I must be willing to let them move and grow, to respond and to wait. And so, the question I must ask myself, whether I am thinking of my own child or my entire company, whether I am leading in my church or serving within my community, is this: Am I willing to be patient with others, or will I simply give up on them? Will I be the kind of leader who walks with people, or runs on ahead? Because though it might feel good to push on to new horizons, you'll find that the farther you are ahead, the less influence you will have. Go too far down the path, out of sight around too many corners, and you'll find you've lost your influence entirely. You'll leave people behind, the very people you want to inspire will be choking in the dust and you won't be helping anyone anymore. So, let's slow down. Let's lean back. Let's hold the vision of God up, like a prism to the sun, so we can all be inspired by God's dream for us all. Let's be truly patient influencers.

Reflection Questions

- Consider the statement "The strength of our patience is tied to the size of our vision." Do you agree? Why, or why not?
- How does a lack of patience affect those we are trying to help?
- Where are you currently feeling impatient? Think of people, organizations, or projects. How can you do a heart-check right now?
- How have people been patient with you? How is God being patient with you right now?

A FINAL WORD

I'm working to overcome these ten barriers in my own life. On some days I am more empathetic than on others. My respect seems to wax and wane with the latest news cycle or conflict, and I can get right stuck on my own way of doing things (which is, of course, the best way!). I can be humble in one conversation and vain in the next.

In truth, I need God's grace activating my life daily, as I wrestle with the kind of person he wants me to be: a loving, patient, grace-filled influencer, with a respect for others that outstrips my preferences and an empathy that outmatches my heart, allowing me to believe that God really is working out his big vision for us all. I can be humbly honest about my own growth while truly growing in my understanding of God's word, will, and world.

If I were to identify my greatest barriers today, I'd say that while I am not perfect in any of the ten, I'm particularly bad at three: knowledge, grace, and patience. Lord, have mercy! Knowing this sets the course for my growth journey, as I keep hauling myself before Jesus and asking him to please help!

But what about you? I know we've covered a lot of ground in this book, but were you able to identify the greatest barriers to your good influence? Is there one or two or four that stand out to you as your most significant challenge? Perhaps there a few areas in which you felt a flush of gratitude to God, because you can see how his work in you has enabled you to grow personally and to help others grow, too?

As we finish, I encourage you to take a step back and ask: where is God calling me to grow, based upon what I've heard? What are the barriers I need to overcome? What has the Holy Spirit be awakening in me? And what am I going to implement so I can respond to his leading?

Go back and skim those specific chapters, paying attention to the reflection questions provided. Ask a friend to discuss it with you, share it with your small group, and write up an action plan.

Thank you for taking the time to read this book—now make that time worthwhile by taking practical, intentional steps to overcome your influence barriers. God is calling you to grow personally so that others can grow exponentially.

And friends, I'm cheering you on. We all are. The people in your life, the churches in which you serve, the staff with which you work—everyone needs you to become the best influencer you can be. Jesus wants that, and so does your world. So, can we all agree? Let's become better at growing good influence, so that together we can see more of God's vision become reality, across every relationship that matters.

ACKNOWLEDGMENTS

• A special thanks to author and friend, Valerie Comer, who offered her support and experience with such generosity, enabling me to get this book into your hands.
• Thanks to Chandler Bolt from Self-Publishing School who finally gave me a blueprint for getting published through his helpful and aptly-named book, *Published.*
• Thanks to Jeff Strong, Laurel Pritchard, and Alan Jones for being my early readers and offering me critical feedback.
• Huge thanks to the members of my book launch team for reading advance copies and sharing my book with others: Mike Bennett, Bonny Bjarnason, Matthew Church, Becky Coons, Doug Crumback, Missy Finlay, Gerald Finster, Eileen Fitzpatrick, Avryll Fuller, Bev Greentree, Judith Greentree, Jenny Judge, Ashley Lemmon, Elsie Lo, Dan Mawson, Dalyce Sather-McNabb, Jason Meidl, Colleen Nahnychuk, Laura Nelson, Jon Plett, Laurel Pritchard, Karl Snyder, Amanda Terpstra, Ken Wiens, and Kirstin Yates.
• Thank you to the three communities in which I've been

privileged to serve: The Grande Prairie Church of Christ and the Erickson Covenant Church, as well as the colleagues and students of InterVarsity Christian Fellowship of Canada. Serving with you shaped who I am, and I am thankful to you all.

• My heartfelt love and thanks to the family who loves me most: My parents and siblings, both biological and by marriage, and above all, Tennille, Ethan, and Micah. You are my greatest influences.

• And to our Triune God of grace, Father, Son and Holy Spirit, in whom I live, move, and have my being. I cannot adequately express my gratitude for your steadfast love for me. It's all for you. To you be all glory, power, and honour.

ABOUT THE AUTHOR

Tom Greentree lives in the Creston Valley of British Columbia where he maintains a small, mixed farm along with his wife, Tennille, and sons, Ethan and Micah. Tom is a graduate of Peace River Bible Institute (Bachelor of Religious Education) and Regent College (Master of Arts in Theological Studies) and pastors the thriving congregation of the Erickson Covenant Church.

Please visit tomgreentree.com to explore more of his thoughts on following Jesus and flourishing in our relationships. To see more of the family and the farm, follow him on Instagram and/or Twitter.

instagram.com/tom_greentree

twitter.com/tomgreentree

Made in the USA
Lexington, KY
16 February 2019